The Magic of Spirit

Sharon Bengalrose

The Magic of Spirit

Copyright © 2016 by Sharon Bengalrose Healing

Published by Bengalrose Healing

Designed by Sharon Barbour

Author - Sharon's spirit inspiration writing team

Book cover illustration – by Chris from www.cimbart.co.uk

Printed in the United Kingdom

ISBN-13:
978-1539407485

ISBN-10:
1539407489

Welcome to The Magic of Spirit,
it is time to open your third eye and
mind to the spirit realm and beyond
my friends.

CONTENTS

The 'Magic of Spirit' has been written by the spirit realm for mankind to see how the divine touch of spirit can change you in an uplifting and positive way. You will be inspired, my friends, by the words in this book, which is full of information and guidance from us on awareness of spirit and the signs we leave for you. Also included is a real true story of a light worker and how spirit guided her journey. We have created inspirational writing, and a spiritual alphabet for you to be guided by in your lives, which can be used in your spiritual churches and centres to help guide and teach others, bringing them to the forefront of their spiritual journeys. These teachings will help them to connect with spirit and find the magical existence that awaits them.

We wish to inspire mankind on your life's journey; our intentions are for you all to discover the spirit within, the pure light beings you were before you came to earth. On earth you have a life path, and while you are on earth your purpose is to find your way to spirit and pure love and light. Your purpose is to work with spirit and bring goodness, love and faith out into your world.

For light workers, teachers and the people amongst you that work in a positive giving environment, like nurses, doctors, carers, the type of people that give out so much and take so little back, our aim is for us to work with all of you as your path walks beside the path of love and light. When you make that spiritual connection, my friends, your world will change and become the world it is meant to be. You will draw in the positive and shed the negative; you will draw in the people around you that need to be there. Do not worry about this, my friends, have trust in us that what is coming is right for you.

As you move forward on this magical journey when you first discover us, you will be amazed at how you will be inspired and inspire others. Some of you will become energy healers, or inspire and heal through messages, and some will be inspired to teach our message. Some of you will go to spiritualist churches or centres to sit and listen to others' philosophy and receive spirit messages, and that might be all you need at this time on your journey on earth. But as you know, when you read this book some of the simple touches from spirit will trigger that divine light within you to search for more links to spirit as you move along your life's path towards the divine light. You all have individual life paths and your connection to spirit will vary; never compare yourself to others, you are all unique, you all have your own path to the divine.

Our advice to you, my friends, is that as you seek a spiritual life and development and surge forward on your life's path with it, you seek out teachers that are well known to develop your spiritual path in a safe way, in prayer and love. There are people amongst you that do abuse this slightly, so it is important to us that we lead you to the correct place to learn, a sanctuary for spiritualism. When you find the correct place you will know it in your heart and you will be welcomed; the people there will only have good in their hearts for you, as we do, my friends. You will then develop on your pathway whatever direction it is for you to take and believe me, we know what that direction is, it's just your task to discover it. You will have paths put in front of you, and your ego and self will help you choose your path; but we do try in our loving ways to lead you onto the right path.

The more you connect to spirit, the more you meditate, the more you tune into us, you will see the signs and see what is needed for you. If you choose to develop your gifts and skills in acknowledging spirit, and receiving messages to pass on to others to help heal and guide them, then you must work hard my friends; you must work with spirit regularly in a safe, protected way to develop this. We love nothing more than a very keen, hard working human who wants to connect with spirit, and we will give our awe in the spirit realm to help you, to lead you on your path to the divine light. Now sit back and enjoy our words, we know you will be inspired.

Chapter 1

The Magic of Spirit is waiting for You All

The key to the magic of spirit is love. The word love is one of our favourite words amongst your languages. Love to us in the spirit realm is pureness of spirit, caring for each other, nurturing, kindness, looking after and protecting each other and being selfless with our love. We would do anything to help our spiritual friends to ascend on their learning and wisdom journey in the spirit realm. We don't have to worry too much about our own welfare in the spirit realm because of the way we lovingly care for each other. When we take our journeys to other planets, realms and dimensions, we learn from what we experience and bring it back to the spirit realm. We discard the negative and only keep the love and positive side to move on with. But we do learn from the negative side of our experiences too.

We see so much love on your earth my friends, but we see especially in the western world, where you have so much media, that love gets forgotten, and this causes a lot of you to forget how much love there is around you. We see among mankind that love can cause elevation and wonder, but it can also cause despair. There are a few ways this can manifest for you - when you find who you think is the true love of your life, and sadly, for whatever reason, that person either departs back home to us or betrays you. We see love bring you down into depression and a spiral of wondering what life is about. Some of you come out of this spiral, some of you find spiritualism and us through it, but others do not find the strength to achieve this on their earth journey at that time on their path. Some of these spirit friends will choose to come back for another journey on earth to achieve this.

Love is the core of all life, for example the love of a newborn child is reflected in the eyes of the mother and father; we see the love in your eyes and hearts, my friends. We see the love for partners, friends and life itself. For you, love is also for your animals and the bond you make with them. A lot of you do care about Mother Earth's wild life and your pets, especially in the western world, and we see the heartbreak it causes you when humans or pets you love pass over.

So what stops you having the love and experience that we have in the spiritual realm? Well, what we call the human essence, a part of the physical form and part of your mind, which is something that has been named your ego. Your ego has the purpose of questioning what you do; it kicks in and stops you feeling the full wonder of love you could experience on earth.

For those of you that have managed to step on the path of love and light and started along it, you will be pushing your ego further back within you and letting your spirit within and spiritual side come forth. When this starts to happen for you, the decisions you make with your mind and heart are from the spiritual realm. My friends, we will be guiding and helping you to hear us more and more when you start this journey.

Love is such a wondrous thing. It is really hard to explain it in a four-letter word, and there are so many parts to it, such as kindness, selfless acts, helping others with no thought of yourself as you push others forward on their life's journey. Love is a wonder to us, my friends, it is so spiritual, and we exist and thrive on it. Love is all to us, and like that divine spark that created us many millennia's ago. We also see love in other beings in other realms and dimensions and there are beings that have managed to ascend to our level. This is quite inspiring to witness, and it is what we want for all of mankind, for all of you to have this love in your hearts and spirit within, to experience no depression or sorrow when you lose someone, as you will know they come back home to us and life carries on for them.

We do see this as a factor in your way of being, your ego feeling the fear of the unknown, and wondering what is beyond. We hear a lot of you say, *There is no after life, when we die this is it*, but when you say it, you always wonder in your inner thoughts if it is really true. So we would like to leave our love with you, my friends. Our love is written in the words of this book to help and guide you and bring you forth on your journeys to find that pure love. We have to admit you will never experience the love you will experience when you return home to the spirit realm, but we can tell you that you can achieve great love on earth if you would just open yourself up to it; let it come in and your life will be changed forever.

The moment you discover spirit for the first time is like no other feeling

4

you will ever experience again in your earth life, as you are touched by the divine love. But some of you, when you first experience this, think it is a fantasy or illusion of your imagination, my friends.

For those who have not yet discovered the pure love of spirit let me take you back to a time in your life when you have seen a magician, a film about magic or read a book and never forgotten that magical moment in the story, lost in the world of the unknown, fantasy and magic where it takes you. Perhaps you have taken the time to sit and watch children absorbed in their play? In their own magical fantasy world, and that moment of pure innocent love of the young you see as they play, it is a magical feeling to capture and experience. Again, if you have been fortunate enough to witness the birth of a child, you will know the overwhelming feeling of love that comes over you, and you cry with joy. These are all close examples of how you will feel when you make that first connection with us.

The magic of spirit is in each and every one of you from that divine moment of our joining with you in your human form on Mother Earth. When the divine spark is ignited and spirit blends with the human body, magic exists. An amazing event of creation, it is no illusion my friends, it is pure true love and light from the divine source.

The magic of spirit lies within you all, my friends; you have it within your inner being, some of you see your spirit as a soul, and we see it as the pure spirit that lies within you. Your soul to us is your integrity, character, wisdom, human essence and our spirit, and all of this makes you who you are in the physical human form.

Why do we call it magic? The magic of the light of the Divine, my friends, the pureness of this high vibration of spirit, is what it can offer you on your life's journey while on the earth plane, or in any other life you choose, on other planets, realms and dimensions. When you find this magic your life changes, and at first, you will notice perhaps small wonderful changes as you progress on your spiritual path. The magic begins to build, but don't expect it to be a complete magical experience all at once, like a big pop of a beautiful firework, and everything will be wonderful for you; that would make your life on Earth just a little bit too easy, as you do have the life path of challenges you have set yourself to experience. Remember you are on the earth for your inner spirit friend to learn and gain knowledge and wisdom.

We also use the word magic when you gain wisdom and knowledge, because you are simply a better person as you grow through spirit on your journey. We are not talking about the knowledge you learn in your schools, in your education, or in your work places. It's the knowledge of life, the universal knowledge, as there is so much more out there for you to discover. As part of the human race, you can just tap into the universal knowledge, and you will find your existence will become more magical.

As we said before in our previous book 'Utopia', you live in a 3D world, my friends, but if you could all just tap into that knowledge and wisdom of the universe, that magical existence out there, you will find your vibrations will rise and your life on Earth will take on a completely new way of being. We have been thinking about the meaning of the word Utopia; it is a place where you can all find your place of perfection, your ideal world, and my friends, this can be achieved for you while on the earth plane. As individuals, you will all have your own opinions and ideas of what Utopia should be, your imagining of it, but mankind can work together, combining all your Utopia concepts to create a magical kingdom. We are thinking of your fairy tales amongst mankind, reflecting people's thoughts and dreams, taking you away from your day-to-day reality, where you read the stories which take you off to a magical place, a place with no worries, a place with love, a place where all your dreams are answered. That, my friends, is Utopia, and you can find this wonderful way of being while here on the earth plane.

When you recognise this spark of the divine in your human life, you are so consumed by the rush of love from spirit that it can make you quite emotional, not quite believing this magical moment. You question that moment in time; did your mind just play a trick on you? Are your feelings real? Did that just really happen to me? Was it an illusion? This is no magic trick; this is when your trust comes into play my friends, because YES, it did just happen to you.

I wish I had a magic wand to wave over you all, so you trusted in spirit. But as mankind has free will, this is often a challenge to us in the spirit realm. The fact you are reading this book means you believe in spirit or are very inquisitive about the spirit realm. If you are not yet working with spirit, what stops you from continuing with this exploration? Is it fear, my friends?

Fear of the unknown, fear of stories other humans have told you of the afterlife - ghosts, culture fears and other experiences they do not understand? Some humans like nothing better than to express their fear and the side of their existence that they have no understanding of, but this is their world, their reality, not yours. They make the fear. Remember there is no fear with the spirit realm; we are pure love and light, working with you to make your existence the best it can be.

Your imaginations over the centuries have written stories of our realm as we allowed you to see glimpses into it. Some of you who believed in us in past times were branded as witches and wizards; their beliefs and actions were seen as magic, the unexplained, ideas feared by mankind.

Throughout mankind's development, different religions have emerged - this is mankind's interpretation of your spirit within and inner power that you have struggled to explain. On the occasions we have shown ourselves we are seen as miracles, and mankind has been given hope in times of despair, recording these occasions in books, with religions developing from these sparks of the divine. But we still hear your voices of despair; you have free will to change your world and yet you choose to still self-destruct with the spark of the divine forgotten. This lesson has not been learned from your past, as your history of wars and conflicts shows us.

We do not intervene very often, in hope that you will learn from these past events. Before you come to earth when you set your life's plan, your main goal is to bring enlightenment to mankind – and oh boy, what a challenge this is for you! When one of you sees the light and asks for help, then we can step in and bring the magic to your world. Until then we watch you travel your life's path, nudging you where we can, leaving magical signs for you to follow, and then bringing you safely home when it is your time to return to us.

We are with you from the moment you are born, to the day you pass back home to the spirit realm; every new baby is born with a pure heart and the magic of seeing spirit. We like nothing better than bringing our spirit friends to your earth; we gather round that spirit and human form from the day they take their first breath, guiding and protecting. We wait for that human to see the love and light on their path, and ask us for guidance, and for us to sprinkle our magic dust down onto you.

The magic of joining and separation with spirit

The joining of spirit with a human form is the beginning of a magical journey. Your spirit comes to earth to join your physical body as a pure spirit, joining with the essence of what you call the human spirit. When the spirit leaves our realm it splits; one part stays with us in the spirit realm, named by yourselves as the higher self.

When the spirit first comes to earth a high percentage stays back in the spirit realm. Your higher self stays with us in your spirit group, always with you, connected by thought and energy. Your higher self converses with your spirit group, which includes your guides, angels, and any other high ascended species here to help you with guidance and healing as you travel your journey on your life's path. All have the collective interest of the best for the wellbeing of your spirit and human form while on earth.

As your earth body grows and develops mentally, more of your spirit gently blends with you until the day you are balanced for your life's work. Have any of you ever said, *I feel sixteen inside even though I'm forty years old*? Or, in my human friend Sharon's case, she always feels thirty-two years old inside, because that's when her spirit balanced. Please understand that this balance is affected by the human energies in your 3D dimension, and the energy of your higher self to connect with these. The timing of the balance will vary depending on your life plan, length of life and the paths you take. Remember that free will and human ego all affect this balance.

Every human is made up of energy matter, and all the vibration frequency patterns of your energies will vary; each one of you, even as a fertilised egg, will vary from each other. We have to balance the vibration frequency patterns of our energies with yours; as you develop these patterns change, so we are adapting all the time, to blend with your physical body and mind connection so that we can maintain a lifelong relationship with you. So if you have an accident, get pregnant, are studying, or feel stressed, all of this affects our blending and you all have a balancing time in your life's path, which will vary.

There are times when the young human form you call a foetus cannot form its energies correctly and the spirit has to separate and come home, as it cannot blend properly to maintain the relationship needed. We know this causes a sadness amongst humans, leaving them wondering what that lost life might have been.

I hear you thinking, *'but we are told our lives are planned, this should not happen, the spirit realm is all knowing and can stop this!'* Yes they are planned, and this joining is a marvelous wonder, but as with all life's forms there is a balance that has to exist to make that connection work. As with all worlds, realms and dimensions we visit, nothing is a hundred percent perfect, not even in the spirit realm, although reflecting on it, we manage ninety nine percent. Remember, the early separation in the end is best for both parties involved and we always try to strive for the perfect reunion with all species we have contact with.

Wow! I know your minds are trying to grasp this. Further facts for you: some of us do plan to enter a physical body that will be what you called handicapped, with some form of disability as you see it in your world. Our journey on these occasions will be for lessons that others will learn around our chosen form, as well as our own humble lessons from this experience.

We know humans can never fully understand, and we know that some of you feel we use the human form to our benefit without much thought to you. You cannot be further from the truth, my friends. We did choose you for your adaptability to our alien energies many, many thousands of years ago, without knowing what to expect. As we started working with humans, we soon learnt that you have an individual essence and personality; this is the best we can describe it. So when we first started to blend with you, this was not much of a challenge. But as your awareness grew, and your intelligence and DNA altered, so did your energies, and we learnt to grow with you. Through this growth of love, we have a strong bond with your Mother Earth and we want the best for ALL mankind. We are fascinated by what is created with our blending, and there is a pure magic in the experience of watching mankind develop to be the best they can. We, as many other off-world beings, want the best for your beautiful planet and are trying to guide you to this goal.

We are often asked what it is like when you die and the spirit leaves your earth body. This transition period is done gently, with lots of support and love from your spirit group, guides and angels. When your spirit leaves your body it can feel what you call a little bit dazed, more so for those that are non-believers. When the spirit leaves it takes its experiences and memories created in that physical lifetime with it, as well as a part of that human essence character we mentioned earlier. When your time of passing is near we start to gather near you, with your higher self more often, sending healing in preparation for the spirit's departure.

At the point your spirit has left the physical form, your spirit still has a strong pull to Mother Earth's energies. Some spirits want to stay a little longer to say good-bye, and travel round their loved ones expressing this. Most of you will not be aware of this, but some of you will pick up on things, such as smelling their perfume, favourite flower or tobacco brand. When the spirit has adjusted to being out of the body, it travels back to our spirit realm with the love and support of its coming home team.

The decision to connect with mankind and blend our beings with yours was made over thousands of years ago in your time. We never take this decision lightly, because it affects and changes a world by changing its future; our intent is always to achieve the best for that planet, realm or dimension, leading its inhabitants to love and light.

As we have said before, we do not force this upon you, but in parts of your cultures, which are indoctrinated in your world by leaders' beliefs, we see you being forced to believe in a way of being that is not right for mankind. The people ruled by such leaders have to obey and live by their rules and religious thoughts and way of being, or they are imprisoned or killed. This has never been the way we have existed; our existence goes back so much further than a few millennia my friends. I cannot find a word in your time that can convey how long we have existed in the Universe. We suppose that if the human race were deciding to blend with another species as we have, it would be of great scientific interest to you. There would be testing and there would be failures until you succeeded in the way you could achieve this. This is what we had to go through as well, failure not as in death, but failures before we could succeed in making the energies blend and work together.

We realised that there were periods of time when other species came to your planet as well, and we did not blend with them while they were there because we only chose the human form. Some of the off-world beings as described in the book 'Utopia' have bred with the human race and created a

10

new gene pool. When this happened to your planet, we adjusted the way we connected with those human beings that had DNA from star people. With every human generation the DNA alters every time, so every time we join with you, we have to make sure we have adjusted in the right way.

In the spirit realm, we have groups of scientist beings and doctor spirit teams that work to ensure that we create the best for all parties concerned while blending. As we have said, we have rare cases when spirit cannot blend properly; even with the best intentions in love and light we cannot be hundred percent, but we are working on it. If only we had a magic wand, as I know your scientists wish they had at times!

So the spirit connects with the human being. As you cannot see the spirit friend that lives within, the question is: where is the spirit in your body? The doubt that comes into the human mind is because it cannot be visibly seen and taken from the physical body while you are living. The spirit sits within your energy. The best way we can explain this is we sit within the core of your body, your inner being, which is not visible to the physical form. Your human form has an essence to it, with structure. Try to imagine a vessel sitting within the body of your physical form like a cylinder, which you cannot see because it is shrouded from you. We live within this inner vessel, connecting to every cell, molecule, nerves, every spark of your physical existence. We connect with your mind, almost as if the spirit has tentacles, but imagine the tentacles as silver threads that go out into your physical form and connect with everything that the spirit needs, as the human body is like a battery for us, enabling us to access your energy.

Imagine the spirit and the silver magical threads as part of you that links to your body. They are connected to the 5th dimension – the spirit form in your body is always on a higher energy frequency. This is why a blending of a spirit with a human has not been as straightforward in the past and has taken us many, many of your centuries to master.

When your time of passing is upon you and your physical form shuts down and dies, the spirit disconnects its silver threads and releases itself back into the universe; guided by some spirit friends, it finds its way back home to the spirit realm. The spirit has what you could call a homing beacon; it knows where to go but we always provide an escort because, as we have said, there are cases when a spirit leaves a physical form and can be slightly confused, so it takes a while for it to adjust. This does depend on the life they lead. For example, a non-believer of life after death will have more of a shock and need reassurance to bring them back home. I know you are thinking, *well, the spirit will know.* YES, but the spirit takes on so much of the physical 3D plane that it cannot shed this straight away; a time of healing is needed when they come back home to shed their physical life and become the spirit they once were.

So my friends, your spirit friend lies within you, connecting to all parts of your body, and running on a higher vibration and it is contained within your physical form. Your spirit sits within you with its own character, own being and own existence. Your new physical body inherits genes from your past, so every time we connect with a human form there is a new beginning, a new being, a new character. We really look forward to this, my friends, to see what develops, what comes from the combination of the two joining and working together.

Your children are born with the magic of spirit within

How many mothers notice their young babies smiling and gurgling at unseen things? When the baby cannot even focus yet and they seem to be smiling and contented at an unseen force? My earth friends, I am a guide to a lady who has recently had a granddaughter. We heard the mother say, *"I think she's smiling at her angels",* and yes, my friends, she was. This is a rainbow child born two weeks before these words were written, and her grandmother is a light worker. Spirit is very strong in the presence of this child, as with all children.

This child picked her parents and grandparents, as they are aware of spirit. The adults around her will not suppress her and her pure spirit will be allowed to develop into the light worker she needs to be – she has great purpose on your earth, as all light workers do.

In the spirit realm we would like to keep this magic of spirit your children are born with, but sadly this is a battle for us, as mankind suppresses this through fear and ignorance. As soon as your children take their first breath, they are influenced by your words, home environment, how you interact with them, what you teach them, your beliefs and the air they breathe.

It's all very well us going on about what you can do, but you do need our help, and we are working behind the scenes my friends, to aid you with your children.

Some of you will have heard of **'Star Children'**. But why the word **'Star'**? The word alone sends magical signs to you of hope for mankind, looking up at the sky; the unanswered questions such as are we alone? And believing loved ones shine as a star in the heavens. These Star Children are beings from the spirit realm and beyond; we work collaboratively with other high ascension beings to be part of this mission. They are being born amongst you to help mankind move forward and evolve. They possess psychic, spiritual and other extra-sensory abilities. These children will bring peace, topple corrupt systems, and shift dimensional consciousness in the years to come.

We have divided them into three categories on your earth to help aid your understanding of them: Indigo, Crystal, and Rainbow Children. These are just words with no meaning to us, but we picked them because for you, they have great meaning. Remember, the Star Children have chosen specific family and friends who will help them develop their natural abilities. So if you are a parent of a child you class as different from the norm, your child chose you to help them, so they can help others on their spiritual path. They have slowly been coming to earth for over a century, but in the last twenty years, there have been lots more. We have increased this because mankind has shifted to accept these children more into their societies and the fifth dimension energy can now filter down more to your third dimensional world.

The Indigo Children: Why **'Indigo'**? Look at the colour, one of the seven colours of your rainbows, a colour of protection to the spirit realm. You will recognise Indigo Children, as they are passionate in their beliefs, whatever they may be, and the strength of their feelings can often be overwhelming for them. These children want to know the truth and want to break down the patterns of traditional thinking. The Indigo Children have a specific purpose, which is to seek out the truth and change archaic systems of thought on the old energy grid, and usher you into a new world of integrity. They are creating a new path and unveiling lies and secrecy to help Crystal Children, who will see the world from an elevated platform of spirituality, and a highly evolved viewpoint with complete and unconditional love. A lot of your Indigo Children will have what are considered to be behavioural problems, which are called Attention Deficit Hyperactivity Disorder (ADHD) and similar labels; this is because they function on a higher frequency and struggle at times to fit into the 3D energy field of earth. These children will be misunderstood by others not on the love and light path, but remember, if you have an Indigo Child, you were chosen as a parent because you will understand your child and guide them towards their desired goal. Remember they are here to create a new energy frequency, and to bring about 'one world', populated by unique, individual, freethinking people living in the fifth dimension.

The Crystal Children: Why **'Crystal'**? Look at your Mother Earth's make-up, which includes beautiful crystals. Crystals are bonded together over time and have great strength. Crystal Children's main purpose is to take you to the next level in your evolution and reveal to you your inner and higher power. They function as a group consciousness rather than as individuals, and they live by the Law of Mankind to be one. They will also be advocates for love and peace on Mother Earth. The first thing you will recognize about Crystal Children is their forgiving nature. They are very sensitive, warm and caring. Don't mistake these characteristics as a sign of weakness, as Crystal Children are also very powerful. They can be multi-faceted and able to see outside the box, yet must also play and find their way in your three-dimensional world, so they do not become isolated and alone. They can also tune into the universe, they have high intuition – a gift from spirit – and you will not be able to hide anything from these children because they are all seeing.

The Rainbow Children: Why **'Rainbow'**? They are created by the reflection of light in water droplets, they are of great beauty, and we use them as signs of spirit being around you, giving hope and comfort. Rainbow Children are coming amongst you more frequently, and their numbers have been building in the last few years. Rainbow Children bring joy and harmony to their families. The Rainbow Child is born to smile, which is accompanied by their huge magical hearts that are full of forgiveness. Rainbow Children are psychic and empathic, having the ability to read people's feelings. This gift is usually revealed as they grow older, when they will become light workers and advocates of our realm. One of their purposes is to complete the final stages of the foundation that the Indigo and Crystal Children have made. All three are connected with inner knowing of their purpose on your earth, their higher selves connecting in the spirit realm as a team. These children are a special spirit force sent in to help you all.

With the energy shift, there will now be more and more star children born to take away your world's pain and help build a world without fear, making Mother Earth the magic place it should be. I have just written a glimpse of this for you; there are books on your earth about these children, written by light workers; please study them and spread the word amongst your societies. This will help you recognise these children and nurture them. But please do not single out these children; they need to grow up in the society they are born into, to complete their life's mission where they are needed.

As well as working with your young, we realise we need to start with the adults, as they influence your children. We are working hard with all mediums, healers, and those of you on a spiritual path, which you call light workers, to spread our messages of love and light. We do this through your spirit circles, spirit churches, holistic healers and trance groups. In your term *light workers*, we include anyone that brings light and love to your world; this will include teachers, life coaches, business coaches, carers, medical workers and those in a role where they can guide and inspire others nearer to the divine light.

We are working to bring guidance to all the parents and teachers to help the development of all children. As you can imagine this is a big task for us, but we love a challenge in the spirit realm. The basic building blocks are:

- o Improving their environment
- o Developing positivity and positive attitudes
- o Meditation and its benefits for all of mankind
- o Helping others as part of day-to-day lives
- o Kindness and selfless acts
- o Developing all children to their full potential

Our aim is to bring our positive, uplifting message to mankind in any way it will be accepted. If mankind can be inspired to make positive changes in their way of thinking, in any area of their lives, this will then spread to other humans in their lives. The key to your future is your children, they will be our advocates in your world, so nurture them and spread our message widely, my friends.

You can be an advocate for the spirit realm

We love it when one of you becomes an advocate for the spirit realm, because what they have learnt on their spiritual path is taken out into your world and taught to others. This is a wondrous thing for us, because it shows the wisdom and the knowledge you have gained on your life's journey. You have gained the confidence to become a teacher and spread our words about the pure love and the divine light from the spirit realm and what we wish for mankind.

We are great teachers in the spirit realm; we base a lot of our existence on the love and light way of teaching, and finding the divine path to walk along. We love to gain wisdom and knowledge, and part of our ascension is learning wisdom and knowledge from the higher ascended beings above us. Then we can start teaching it to the spirits sitting in our lower levels, which is how we all learn and progress. As you are aware, you cannot teach anything of which you do not have knowledge, and you need to experience it for yourselves, my friends. When you teach, it should come from not just your mind, but your heart and spirit as well. The pupils that sit in front of you need to be able to see your passion, hear your experiences, and see you have lived what you have talked about. A boring teacher to his pupil in a school will be someone that has just learnt from text books but has never gone and studied the subject in its natural environment. For example, teaching a language and studying it in its country of origin, or studying geography from books and maps without ever going to mountains, rivers, oceans and valleys to see how true geography lies on your earth.

The teachers that have stepped out of the classroom, experienced their subject at first hand, and combined it with their text book learning, will be the most inspired. This is what we do in the spirit realm; we do not teach anything that we have not experienced. This is one of our key values, and is what we would like to see in our advocates among you humans who teach the spirit experience and words of wisdom to others.

So to be a spiritual teacher, my friends, you have to walk the path, and sit with other teachers in circles and workshops to learn. Absorb the wisdom and knowledge and ask the spirit realm to lead you to where you need to be on your teaching journey. There are various spiritual areas you can teach.

Once you have discovered your path you can then take it into your heart and learn everything you can about it, and then, my friends, you can go out and inspire others.

We are now seeing this amongst you more and more, especially in the last twenty years, as you become more aware of spirituality. In the last three to four years where the energies have shifted more and more, and more of you are becoming aware of spirit, more of you are going out teaching the spiritual way of being and also becoming healers. Through this, more humans are connecting with the spirit realm and they are being led on their path to your teachers. This is an awesome thing for us to see, a beautiful thing for us to see, and we do love this part of your journeys and ours in the spirit realm.

We wish you well with your teachings, my friends. Have the confidence to go out there and shine amongst the other lights, and the light of every pupil you connect with will shine brighter too. Every word you speak will shine into their hearts and give them the confidence to move forward on their spiritual journeys.

Connection from within

Take your mind and look within. What do you see?

Do you see the mist of times gone by lying within?

Do you see sunbeams breaking through the clouds?

Do you see a beautiful existence of love and light?

Do you see shadows and flickers of distant hope?

Do you see doubt and a lost spirit within?

To find what lies within your inner being, you need to sit in the silence, my friends, and focus on your inner essence and spirit. Your spirit carries its history for all of you to rediscover while on this earth plane. When you connect truly to this inner being that lives within, all the shadows, doubts and mistrust will be forgotten. The light will shine in, bouncing you forward on your true path to find kindness, love and the faith of the divine.

Remember, as you connect to your inner being, we are all here celebrating with you, only a touch away for guidance and the love you need while on this exciting journey on earth.

My friends, celebrate your wonderful journey with spirit, and take this out to the world, teach and inspire so others can connect with the spirit being that lies within them.

The magic of you

We would like every human to experience being YOU. The true you is the human essence blending with the spark of pure spirit, and you recognise this and shine through. We would like to call those who have achieved this the light ones. For those of the human race that have achieved this wholeness, we see you radiate love, compassion, empathy, positive vibrations, honesty, laughter and a generosity beyond words. As we look down, the true light ones of you shine like a beacon, and you stand out from the crowd.

More and more beacons of light are appearing round Mother Earth. The light ones have already travelled quite a way down their light worker's journeys path. They have shed the humans that cannot serve their journey and they have attracted in the ones that can. They will keep developing, growing on their journey until they return home to us.

The phrase *"I wish I had a magic wand"* is often heard amongst you, my friends. The magic wand is you, the human essence and inner strength we so admire; combine this with our pure spirit, and you will conjure up all sorts of magic tricks. So wave your magic wand, my friends, and connect with us, and TRUST we will guide you on your life's path.

Chapter 2

Capturing the Magic of Spirit

A crystal ball sits on a table, cradled in the hands of the fortune-teller, reflecting the room around it with a mist to its inner depths; an object, used as a way to connect to the spirit realm for messages and guidance. In the human mind, we often find that an object is needed to help you feel secure when working with us, or to serve as a showmanship piece when giving your messages. The onlooker sees the object and believes it is bringing forth the magical communication. But those of you who work with us know that the source of these messages is us blending with your energies, and our thoughts connecting with your mind. The object gives a mystical feeling to the reading – but does the onlooker need this object? Does the reader need it? I would say, my friends, that the answer is no, you just need to trust that we are there with you. Have the confidence you will receive the correct message and guidance that is needed on the day. You can achieve this with trust, and your recipient will hear the message and know it is from us, because the confidence and belief you have in the spirit realm will be reflected in your voice. Every message you deliver will leave no doubt in their minds of the truth and power of spirit.

Through your centuries there have been items used to capture spirit, items designed to protect humans from spirit, and items believed to strengthen your link with spirit. Religious symbols reflect this – the Christian or Catholic cross, Mala prayer beads, a rosary or the bible held in your hands at a time of prayer; the idea behind these objects is that they can help you connect you to the higher realm, where your prayer will be listened to. The cross has also been a symbol of protection to ward off dark spirit in your past history. Icons such as religious carvings of saints, Buddha or the Virgin Mary serve as objects for you to pray to.

In your places of worship, you also have altars or shrines, each of which reflects the beliefs of their religions. Altars serve as a focal point for ceremonies such as weddings, funerals and communion, and they are found in religions all over the earth, as statements of religious beliefs and in some cases, wealth. Shrines give people purpose, mental connection or a relationship linked to the person or object of worship. Some shrines are set in locations where an important event took place, dedicated to a specific figure of worship. These shrines hold relics, where offerings are made and prayers offered up to the heavens. We recognise that these physical objects give people purpose, mental connection or relationship to their chosen icon or belief system, as they are worshipping something they cannot see.

We understand why mankind's healers and mediums use items like crystals, cards, crystal balls and Ouija boards, and other items for connecting to the spirit realm. We are happy to work with you on this basis, because the human part of you needs this safety net, this link that you think helps connects you to us. In the three-dimensional world you live in at the moment, the fear of failure and lack of trust is one of the reasons why you still use these objects. You know inside to trust that we are there, but you feel you need some sort of solid connection to us because you don't see our spirit realm. We have also realised that the clients who come to you looking for a voice of a loved one or some healing, will feel more at ease if they see you using essences, crystals, cards, pendulums or whatever it is you have been drawn to use. Because some clients don't understand about spirit, they see the connection of the items you are using, or believe that the item is bringing forth the source that is making them feel better. This is fine, as it is their way of thinking; they will still get what they need from us, because we're not going to say, *"Oh no, sorry, you can't have this healing or message, because we know you can achieve this without using any of these objects."*

But what we would like to say to you is that you can connect to spirit with trust, with no fear and with the right intent of healing and love for all your clients; we will work with you, so that the person in front of you will receive exactly what they need without you needing any objects. This is because we use your energy field to bring forth our energy, bringing it through your hands to your client so it can heal their body and clear the negative energy areas that need shifting. Your trust will help you sense when we tell you that enough is enough, and it's time to stop the healing session. Through trust, message givers such as mediums will receive the information and guidance needed for a client. So, my friends, we feel that at the moment, yes, this is the way you need to work, using these objects. But we know that as mankind ascends on its journey through the next few generations, these items will no longer be needed, because you will understand that all you need is your mind and energy to connect to us.

We would like to point out that crystals have a power of their own and you are right to assume they have an individual power, of which the spirit realm has made mankind aware. Crystals also have a way of recording and holding information and energy, so that's why it is important they are cleansed regularly if you use them on your clients as a form of healing connection. We do use them to help channel into a human body if available; the human healing source places a crystal and through their hands, we use the crystal to enhance and divert our energy. But as you've probably guessed, we don't need them, as we control where the energy goes for healing. We are happy to carry on along this path with you using your objects, but at the same time, we encourage you to take the plunge and try your message and healing without them, trusting in your connection with us. Remember, you all have healing guides and angels waiting to help you with this.

Every medium and healer works in a different way with different objects, but this does not matter, as what is important to us is every message you give, opens up a light in the heart of the person receiving your help, bringing them a step nearer to spirit. Because we are trying to help you ascend and become better humans, we need to make you aware of this.

We also understand that humans do need objects to see or hold onto when praying, because most of you have not allowed yourself to open up to see and feel the divine spirit. A lot of you sit and worship for a long time, but you have not truly connected to the source. My friends, we do hear your prayers, but your barriers stop the changes you want to make for yourself and the world. Find your true self, change your way of being, shift into the positive higher vibration, and the answers you seek through prayer will come to light.

We are intrigued by the history behind mankind's objects you use for mediumship and healing, you will be surprised at how long they have been in place. For your interest, we have included some here for you from your earth's books.

Candles - They have been a symbol for mankind for centuries, used in religions, celebrations in life, and simply for giving light in a home. Imagine the magic of that first flame, and the discovery of wax and a wick. Picture the magic of this event in your time line, developing these things that then led to these life-changing events. Candles have been used for light and to illuminate mankind's celebrations for more than 5,000 years. The Egyptians were using wicked candles in 3,000 B.C; the ancient Romans were developing the wicked candle before that time, by dipping rolled papyrus repeatedly in melted tallow or beeswax. The resulting candles were used to light their homes, to aid travellers at night, and in religious ceremonies. The use of candles soon spread to more advanced cultures, with candle making techniques evolving over time.

Think: when you discover spirit, your vibration/energy is lifted, and this sends out a beacon of light into the darkness of time, like a candle. Humans believe candles are believed to help draw in spirit, and they are also a symbol of memory at a loved one's parting. When a candle is lit with this intent, it lets the spirit realm know you're thinking of them. But we do not need this object; as we know, the candle is for the comfort of the human essences, and the hope that the departed spirit knows. Trust us – we do.

Crystal ball - Crystal gazing was commonly practiced by your earth people the Pawnee, the Iroquois, the Incas, the Egyptians, the Persians, the Chinese, and the people of Yucatan. These first adopters of crystal gazing would stare deeply into the stone, falling into a meditative trance that would allow the subconscious to open up to give messages, healing and guidance.

The act of gazing into a reflective or translucent surface to glean prophetic insight came to be known as scrying, and the practice was used on literally anything, including blood, water and mirrors, although crystal balls are the most common mechanism for this type of connecting with the divine.

The early crystal gazers, or specularii, preferred a sea-green mineral called Beryl, which was polished into spheres to enhance its reflective properties, the start of the crystal ball. The crystal ball has appeared across the world in various shapes and form, but the one to which you mostly relate in the western world is the image of a woman, usually thought to be a "gypsy," travelling in their caravans and delivering messages to whoever would listen, for the price of a coin crossing the palm.

Pendulum – The pendulum has been used by your healers and mediums for a long time through your history. Historically, it has also been used for dowsing and has been known for its ability to locate water, gold, oil and other minerals, and is still used to this day in parts of your world. But we would mainly like to talk about the use of the crystal pendulums used by healers and mediums today.

They are often used to pick up areas within the human body that need healing, by connecting with a break in good energy flow. The healer connects with their healers in spirit, who work with them and guide them to where their hands should be placed. You can also trust and use your hands; we will give you sensations to pick this up if you do not wish to use the pendulum. But trust, and we will guide your hands to where we need them to go.

Some use the pendulum to connect to the spirit realm as confirmation in your life's looking for yes and no answers. We put a word of caution round this, if you are not protected and using it with out good intent, spirit that are still earth bound or other unseen forces you do not yet understand will be drawn to you, they will play with it and can give false information, so be careful my friends.

Incense - When ancient mankind discovered fire they realised that when burnt, most materials give off a unique and sometimes powerful aroma. The difference between the smell of a handful of leaves and that of a pine tree branch is greatly emphasized when each is burnt. There is historic evidence in most of your earth cultures that people used incense burning for sacred, cleansing and healing purposes. From ancient times, people recognized that aromas produced by burning materials could heighten the senses, both sight and smell. When early man gathered around their fires, the smell of aromatic woods, herbs and leaves carried by heavenwards spirals of smoke was a rare sensory pleasure. A lot of them developed this as a way of worshipping their gods.

They discovered that the benefits of burning incense included the purification of an area, to change a mood to facilitate meditation or religious practices, and to cleanse living spaces after death or illness. Also used today as a practice of protection called smudging, where healers and mediums cleanse a space of negative energy and spirit. Again, my friends, this can be done with prayer; it is the intent of healing, love and light that clears these negative energies.

Dream catchers magic - The magic of thought in the human mind can change the way you are, the way you think and what can happen to you. You do create your own reality, but a lot of humans through the centuries have needed symbols or objects to help trigger these thoughts and positive vibrations. It was also believed that the dream state could bring in mad energies causing nightmares.

A great example of this is the dream catcher, which was created by the Ojibwe people. Stories from your old times speak of the Spider Woman, known as Asibikaashi; she took care of the children and the people on the land. Eventually, the Ojibwe Nation spread to the four corners of North America and it became difficult for Asibikaashi to reach all the children. So the mothers and grandmothers would weave magical webs for the children, using willow hoops and sinew, or cordage made from plants. It was believed the dream catchers would filter out all bad dreams and only allow good thoughts to enter their minds.

These dream catchers are still used today to magic away bad spirit, or so it is thought!!! But it is your own minds that set the thoughts and events that create unhealthy sleep patterns in your 3D world. The dream catcher is just a symbol of something mystical which is thought to magic away bad dreams. You focus on the object, which helps to clear your mind and aids more restful sleep. If you learn to clear your minds, focus, and lift your vibration to the love and light within spirit, restless sleep and the bad dreams will fade and no longer exist for mankind.

Cards – A lot of psychics and mediums use cards for giving messages. They become familiar with a pack they are drawn to, using the beautiful images and symbols on them as triggers for messages and their meanings. Again, we have worked with you to use the cards, the symbol having the basis of a message which helps open your mind to us, so we can then feed in what we have to say to you. We see two sides to you using cards. First of all – yes, you've guessed it – you don't need this prop, it's a comfort tool to hide behind. But we are wise enough to realise that people are drawn to these readings, and the reading given can be a trigger point on their spiritual path, as with all the objects we have mentioned.

Ouija boards – Ouija boards have been around for almost two of your centuries; they were very popular at one time, used by mediums in the western world as a way of demonstrating a physical way of communicating with the spirit realm. We give you a word of caution about this way of communicating: if it is not done in prayer and protection, you open the power of your thought to all out there in the energies of earth. This includes energies not of the spirit realm, from other dimensions, and the layers of unseen forces that surround Mother Earth. This is a similar warning we gave with the pendulum; with this method, you could get false messages and things happen that you cannot control, and do not have the experience to handle. When you need to communicate with the spirit realm, my friends, use a renowned medium.

Signs from the spirit realm

There is only love and light in the spirit realm, my friends, and nothing to fear. We are around you all your life, but many of you stay unaware of us because of mankind's indoctrinated behaviour. Or if you see a glimpse into our realm, you pull away through the fear of the unknown. Many of your religions portray us as evil, or the devil, but we are just an unseen force you do not yet understand.

Over the centuries, most of you have had your pure love of spirit squashed, but in the last 20 years, a lot of you are stepping forward, not afraid to say you believe in the spirit realm. There are more light workers and positive vibrations on Mother Earth now, allowing us to make a better connection with you all. A great shift is occurring, slowly gaining in power, and our aim is to build on this to take you from the 3D dimension, stepping into the 4th, leading you to the 5th. For those of you that do not know, I would like to explain about the Dimension levels.

Mankind lives in the third dimension at the moment; this is a busy, chattering dimension with fear and feelings of powerlessness and loss in the world. You feel you want to do more for your world, but you are swimming against a heavy current, living in hope the tide will change. The third dimension has now served its purpose, with mankind coming to the point where you can now lift yourselves out of it. When we talk of meditation, connecting with your suppressed powers and reaching enlightenment, this is so you can raise your vibrations and awareness to what we call the fifth dimension levels.

The fourth dimension is what we call the middle ground, the stepping-stone to the fifth. The fourth dimension is smoother flowing, offering possibility, capability, and more hope to mankind. You are already starting to work in this dimension with the shift since your year 2000. Since around 2012, the shift has accelerated and there are notable changes in mankind and its attitude to spiritual changes. The more of you that lift your vibration, the more of you will be transported to the fourth dimension way of thinking and being. Your earth will become more enlightened and then the shift will really be moving along at a fast pace.

The fifth dimension exists in a permanent state of peace, bliss, love and joy, where you will also begin to automatically feel love for everyone. No more negative thoughts will stream into the mind of a being who has reached fifth dimension consciousness. Your mind is quieter, allowing for telepathic skills; you will be without the constant chatter that flows into the third dimension mind. While in this wonderful fifth dimension, you can also connect to the universe knowledge pot. You've probably guessed by now in which dimension level we exist. Mankind can exist at this level on earth in your human form, if you lose your layers of doubt and fear. There is a lot of information in your earth's knowledge about this subject, which will fascinate you. The veil is being lifted off Mother Earth so you can shift into the higher dimensions, which is what many of you tuned into spirit are now feeling. We are very busy working behind the scenes to help take mankind into this level of ascension.

When we say a shift is occurring, the layers between the realms are very thin at the moment, and this allows us to channel 5D energy to your 3D level to help you along. Being the middle platform, the fourth (4D) dimension is there to help you to take the next leap of faith and TRUST.

We have always sprinkled magic signs all around you to let you know spirit is present. With the energy shift, you are becoming more aware of them. Ask for your signs to come to you and try to be specific. But be aware when you have lost a loved one, because grief is a very strong emotion; it holds you to the past and stops you living in the present. You become so absorbed with these strong emotions that your heart closes to divine messages. We see grief stricken humans going to mediums for readings; they only want to hear from that one human they are grieving over. This affects their experience as they then block out all other spirit and messages that could help them. They want so desperately to hear from their loved ones, but they cannot see the signs their spirit guides leave them. These feelings change with time; as their grief subsides, they will start to feel their loved ones near and will be comforted.

There are also the scientific ones amongst you that block us through your way of thinking, but again, when you have a strong sign you cannot ignore and cannot give any earthly explanation for, this can trigger you to grasp your spirituality and then break down the barriers. Due to humans blocking us through emotions or ego, we sometimes give our loving comforting messages to others close to them to pass on. When you receive a sign, it will be another magical moment for you to experience in your lives. We have listed below some signs you can ask for or may experience when we are near.

The magic meaning of signs from the spirit realm

Feathers

Finding feathers is a sure sign spirit is around you, and one of the commonly known signs of the angels, guides and loved ones passed over. Feathers of any colour are a beautiful reminder that we are near, loving and supporting you from behind the scenes. When you find feathers in an unusual place, this is an especially powerful sign from the spirit realm.

White Feather - When you find white feathers, they're always a sign from your angels or loved ones in spirit … even when you're in a place where birds are present. They simply mean, *'I am around you, everything will be ok.'*

Black Feathers - Most often found during times of crisis or transition. Usually, you are already having problems and the black feather is a sign from spirit they are aware of your current life difficulties, and helping and supporting you. Ask us for guidance and watch out for more signs.

Yellow Feathers - The spirit realm is saying, *'Congratulations to you! Things are going well right now.'* A positive sign for you to keep, and thank the spirit realm for the good things in your life.

Pink Feathers - A sign your spirit team and angels are joining in with the fun in your life and they will laugh with you but never at you. When you rejoice, we rejoice.

Blue Feathers - This colour is for protection and a time for calm and peace in your life. Find space in your life for serenity by taking a walk by water or meditating. You have to take the steps to make this calm in your life happen; ask us to help you make the space you need.

Red Feathers - Finding a feather with red on it means that we are helping with matters of the heart, and helping you to find passion and love in your life. We like to help you with your modern ways, for example a lot of you now use dating sites to seek love; when doing so you can ask us to guide you to the right person.

Green Feathers - This is a sign your guides and angels use to send you healing, and guidance to ensure you take good care of yourself spiritually and physically. A green feather can also indicate that it's time for you to slow down and concentrate on number one, YOU.

Grey Feathers - Your spirit team and angels are working behind the scenes on the problem that is worrying you. Be ready for our signs soon, watch out for our guidance, and be patient while we put things into place for you.

The meanings of feathers with different colour combinations

Black and white feathers represent protection, or the sense of a union. The contrast of the black and white shows you have some internal conflict over a problem at the moment; give all your worries to us and be kind to yourself.

Black mixed with purple represents a very deep spirituality. Your third eye is getting stronger, so work harder with us and all will become clear for your life's path.

Black, white and blue mixed feathers denote change on the horizon. The blue indicates we are placing protection and guidance around you to help with this transition period.

Brown and black is a sign you are achieving balance between the physical and the spiritual in your life.

Brown and white is for happiness, and a sign that you are being protected from harm. We are protecting your mental and physical well-being.

Feathers with red and green in them, or together, is a sign you are being assisted financially and we are bringing abundance to your life as a whole. This is a very lucky sign

Grey and white symbolise hope for you; there is transition-taking place and your future is not set. You can make the changes needed with us walking beside you, ask us for guidance and more signs.

Coins

The human phrase 'pennies from heaven' does not mean we are showering you with money; it has become a common saying because coins, usually pennies, are often found in obscure places when you are thinking about loved ones. We like to use signs that we know you will recognise, and a small coin is easier for us to handle. The coins can have deeper meaning, so if you come across one, look at the date; does it having meaning for you? Always be assured, coins are deliberately placed on your path to show we are with you offering love, support and guidance.

Rainbows

We love using rainbows to make you pause and wonder at the beauty of Mother Earth. This is also a sign from the divine that we are with you. They are shown to you at times you need reassurance in your lives, and they offer you hope and comfort.

Clouds

We do have fun using clouds as signs that we are near, and I'm sure you have seen earth images of the angel shapes we show you. We also use other images in the clouds that have meaning to you at that time. So look up to the sky, my friends, and while you are cloud gazing, be open to the images we send you.

Birds

We often use the robin as a sign from spirit, as it's a very popular bird amongst you and is often seen all year round in parts of your western world. Where there are no robins, we choose a bird of beauty that resonates with someone as a sign that spirit is near.

Butterflies

These are such beautiful creatures that reflect the beauty of your world. We love to use butterflies as signs from the spirit realm as they signify transformation across many of your cultures on earth. The butterfly represents the inner spirit that has been released from the physical form. If you have been thinking of a loved one or asking for guidance, and a butterfly lands on you, or near you, know we are close and have heard your prayers.

Speaking to you, repetitive words, numbers and images

We give you lots of signs but we can also give verbal warnings, which may sound like a voice next to your ear or in your head. These are used to protect you on your life's path in the hope you heed us. With light workers, we also use signs such as repetitive words, numbers and images, because they have already acknowledged us and work with us; they are open to the signs and will be looking out for them. We do also use them with the rest of mankind, usually when we think you will see them; even if you don't understand it, it would be at a profound time in your life. There are earth books written about these number sequences that have the meanings from spirit and their messages for you.

Dreams

Spirit can use your dream state to give you guidance and show we are OK after we have passed. When you sleep your vibration changes, your five senses slow down, and your sixth sense is given a chance to shine. You will find these dreams will be more vibrant than others and of course you will remember them. Some of you describe them as a waking dream, an experience you will rarely forget.

The gap between earthly reality and the spiritual world changes during sleep, allowing us to enter your mind, and your subconscious is open to ideas that your rational minds would not normally see or allow. We suggest you have a notebook by the bed, so you can remember any dreams and record ideas that come to you, they will change your life for the better.

Movement of objects

We do like to have a bit of fun, especially our young spirits, and move objects when you are not looking, then when you least expect it, the object will re-appear again. If you notice this happening and you do not like it, just ask us to stop and we will; this will tell us that you have at least seen our sign and are aware of your spirit friends. Or just ask us to return the object because you need it, it is all done in love and fun.

Scents

This is a very popular method for us to give signs that we are around you. It will be the scent of a favourite perfume or flower that a loved one wore while on earth. We also like to use tobacco and cooking smells associated with your loved ones too.

Temperature change

When spirit is near you and they come close to comfort you, you might experience a change in temperature; can be a coldness you feel or you might feel hot and flushed - this is all normal. It happens as we make contact with your energy field; the vibration from the spirit realm can slow or speed up the molecules in the air, resulting in a change in temperature. Every person will vary in how they react to our interaction with them. If you are in acceptance of this contact just go with it; if not, just ask us to stand back. You can always ask us to draw nearer when you are ready. Remember you are always in control.

Music

Spirit love to use music for a sign or a message to you. You might hear a choir and not be sure where the singing comes from. You might be thinking about a passed loved one and their favourite song comes on the radio, or a song that had meaning around that person. If you hear a repeating song, listen to the words, ask spirit why you keep hearing it, and the first thing that comes into your head will be the answer.

Voices

Babies and animals have not yet taken on many of the filters, which can block your ability to clearly see your guides, angels or a member of your spirit family dropping in to say hello. Have you ever noticed a baby looking up smiling at what seems to you empty space? Or perhaps your pet's focus is captured by something you are unable to see; your dog's tail happily wagging at an unseen force. Yes, they are seeing and hearing our spirit realm. In the presence of their spirit team and spirit group visitors, babies, small children and animals will be at ease, showing signs of comfort and excitement.

We also use voice communication to adults to make them aware of spirit; quite often this is their first link to acknowledging us. It can sound like voices in the next room, or whispers; you cannot quite hear what they are saying, but when you reach the room it stops. Few of you are blessed with hearing us directly, like a person standing next to you; you will all mostly hear our thoughts in your head telepathically, as we draw into your energy field. But we would like to say as mankind ascends you would all hear us clearly one day.

Different coloured lights

Shafts of light streaming or shooting around you are definite indications of the spirit realm. Don't be afraid if you notice sparks of light or shadows around you. The digital technology you now use can capture orbs, signs that spirit energy is near you. Spirit don't want to harm you, this is normally a sign that they are trying to reach you directly. If you do not work with spirit and you think spirit are trying to contact you, seek out a recommended medium to see if they have a message for you.

Touch

We do like to draw close to your energy and touch your head, arms or hands to comfort you or give you healing. You might feel a tingle, or the sensation that something has just brushed your skin. This is a gentle touch of love and healing for you, it will give you comfort without you really knowing why.

Chapter 3

How the Magic of Spirit can Change your Lives

My light worker's journey and awareness of spirit

I was asked by Harold and his team to write about the magic of my light worker's journey. I could not understand this request at first, or why my spiritual journey would be of interest to anyone. Then I took my first workshop, where I taught and shared some of my experiences and what I have learnt from working with spirit and other spiritual teachers. I saw people leave my workshop smiling, saying lovely things about their day, after being inspired by what we had said and sharing our knowledge.

So I now think back at my life and wonder, where did my journey begin? It started with me sitting down with my spirit group in the spirit realm choosing my parents, brothers, husband, children and friends. Setting my life's path goals and experiences, and then down I came with the seed inside me to spread love and light. May I add that this seed is in all of us, waiting for some moment in our life to germinate and grow, spreading out beauty and magic as we connect with spirit.

As I write this, I have just been reminded that as our spirit comes down, we experience a division, leaving our higher self up with our spirit groups. As our human body grows, more and more of our spirit filters down to the point of a split that balances our spiritual needs.

I chose my birth mother, who was unmarried, and a father that did not want to know when she became pregnant with me; this was already her chosen path. My birth mother had to give me up for adoption, as her family could not accept me into their home back in the 1960s. I was born in a home for unmarried mothers, which was run by nuns, and was placed for adoption in an area where my adoptive parents had moved. My adoptive father was in the RAF and had just transferred to the area where I was born. My adoptive mother had lost some children, and it was advised she had no more. But they did have one natural son, and my adoption added to their family. My adoptive parents were then blessed with another natural son, and after that my adopted mother had a hysterectomy.

And so my earth life had started. I was not aware of spirit until about the age of eleven, I just knew something was different, in my looks, what I liked and the way I thought. I was told I was adopted at a young age and nothing was hidden from me. I accepted this as the reason I was different. I had a happy upbringing in the first few years and I now look back I realise that changes started to happen in my family unit when I was around the age of 11. My father was a teacher by this time; I was in his school and class and got teased and bullied as result, which really affected me for a couple of years. My mother went to study for a degree and was not at home much; at this time we got an au pair for a while. It was an unsettled time for a child, but as with most things, we adapt.

It was also at this time that I became aware my parents were heavy drinkers. Why mention this to you? Well, all our experiences, good or bad, influence and contribute to who we are today. I won't put down all my personal experiences of family life and how it affected me as an individual, as I could go on forever, so I will concentrate mainly on just my spirit and alien experiences.

My first experience of spirit was around this time. We went on holiday and stayed in an old cottage. When we pulled up outside the cottage I remember looking at the building and feeling frightened; it felt as if I was being watched. As we entered the front room I remember feeling uncomfortable, but the real feeling of fear was in the dining/kitchen area. I sensed that something had happened there and knew it was to a woman who had lived there. I was supposed to sleep downstairs on my own, being the only girl, but I got so upset, I slept upstairs with my younger brother and there, I did not feel any fear. My elder brother slept downstairs; he felt uncomfortable too, but did not react like me. I was lucky my parents seemed quite open to the idea of spirit, so I wasn't told I was being silly.

Years later, after my father died, I was clearing out his photos and I came across a picture of the cottage. All the feelings I had experienced at the time came flooding back to me. I could not keep the picture, as the memory was one I did not want to be reminded of.

My second unusual spirit experience was when I was fourteen. My older brother, now eighteen, was looking at going to university in Southampton. My mother took him down to visit and I went too. While he was looking around the university we went shopping. As I was walking along the high street, I froze; it was as if I had gone back a hundred and fifty years or more and I knew I had been there before. I saw similar buildings, carts and carriages, a muddy road with straw. I also remember a well-to-do lady with a slave child in tow. Next thing I heard was my name being called by my mother; the memory of that day never left me. I did often wonder if I had imagined it, but I know now it was a glimpse of what I believe was a past life existence.

Well, my brother went to Southampton University and I really missed him, as he was my rock at home. I realised by this time I had a very controlled upbringing; for example I was told, *"You must join the young conservatives"* and *"Don't mix with coloured people."* I felt very out of place as this was not the way I felt or thought - these were my parents' words and ideas. Both my parents were very strict and controlling but my mother more so. I now realise that they had had similar upbringings and believed this was the correct way to bring us up. This did affect the emotional side of my being, which manifested when I got postnatal depression with my second child; I was told I had been mentally abused as a child and young adult. Due to my holistic healing and journey with spirit, I have released my hurt and fears and hold no malice towards my parents. I feel a bit guilty revealing this about them, but it was all our life path journeys interacting to make us what we need to be. I will reveal that my father has been through from spirit and told me he loved me and wished he had shown me more love while he was with me. I sat and cried, I needed to hear it.

I did follow my parents' wishes back then and through this, I met some religious friends. I discovered Jesus at seventeen, hippie skirts and a guitar, I loved singing Jesus songs and went to places where groups talked in tongue; it was fascinating. But all through my life I had never felt comfortable with churches, and it seemed that religion was fear based, which did not sit well with me. At this time, I also had a very good friend who asked me to do a Ouija board at her house with our friends. She lived in an old house that I sometimes felt uneasy in. I refused point blank, and could not leave the house quick enough. Even today, I still hear a voice telling me to stay away from Ouija boards.

My journey with Jesus carried on for a year or so until one day, myself and my best friend at the time decided to try out a new church. We turned up for the service, but were diverted off to a side room, and asked if we were willing to get on our knees to confess our sins before we could join. My alarm bells started ringing, telling me to get out of there! Well, I legged it with my friend, and that is when I took a step back from religion.

My first UFO experience was in this time period too. One day in my hometown of Loughborough, I was walking towards town when I looked up and on the distant tree line, saw a pulsating light object moving slowly. I thought it was a small plane, then it suddenly darted back and forth, then darted quickly to the right, hung in the sky for a while, then shot off at high speed and disappeared. One of my 'did I imagine it' moments - but I knew I had not. That week in the local paper, UFO sightings were reported. I had always known aliens were out there and could never explain why; it was just in me and I was always fascinated by UFO stories.

At the age of nineteen I went to Art College in my hometown of Loughborough. This was the day my life changed. I discovered just how controlled and sheltered my upbringing had been; all of a sudden I was mixing with all nationalities and cultures – and I loved it. I found I could have my own opinions and not be afraid to voice them. This did not go down well at home and this is when changes in my home life took a turn for the worse as I started to find out who I truly was at long last. Looking back, my parents had wanted to get me into an academic private school but I was not very academic like my brothers; instead I was very creative, and they really had no choice but to let me go this art route, which took me to a comprehensive school, then the Art College that changed my life.

This life-changing year is when I had my third spirit encounter. I got a job in a pub and worked in the public bar. Where I stood waiting to serve people was a narrow space and for people to get by me, I had to move out of the way. I had been working there for a couple of weeks when one night I felt two hands on my hips and I was gently pushed out the way; imagine my shock when no one was there. I made some inquiries and the landlord told me they had had some activity in my bar area and kitchen since they had done some building work upstairs in the pub. I left the pub as I needed to get a job nearer my college, but this memory never left me.

The first year at Art College was an emotional life changer for me. My parents had told me when I was seventeen that they wanted me to marry a doctor or dentist and never to bring home a coloured man. I realised at that point they were snobs and racist, not my way of being at all. Well, I discovered later that I did the next worst thing in their eyes, when I brought home a nineteen-year-old boyfriend with long hair, tie-died clothes washed in the student clothes boiler, and a motorbike. We were in love; in my eyes, he was the nicest chap you could meet. Sadly, my parents did not take to him and told me to choose them or him, so I left home one day and never went back; we became estranged, and my life carried on without much contact with them.

I married my longhaired biker and we bought our first home. This is where I experienced my fourth spirit encounter. We bought an old terraced cottage that we nicknamed The Refresher Row, as all the houses were painted in the colours of the sweets; ours was pink. I didn't notice anything for the first few months, then we put stairs into the basement and started renovating it. I started to have dreams, or waking moments of seeing someone standing at the top of the landing looking into our room. He was dressed in middle class Victorian clothes, with dark collar length hair and a hat. A couple of times, I felt as if I was being held down in the bed or someone was leaning over me. There were also times when my two cats would follow something with their eyes, then dart out of the cat flap at high speed. Sometimes, when I sat playing at our piano, I felt someone was behind me, watching. My husband never felt or saw anything. I only told one other person, a friend at work, as it played on my mind. Then one day an old friend came to stay; I had not told her of my gentleman spirit visitor. A few months later I went to stay at her house and we were talking about ghosts etc, and she said, 'you know you have one? I saw him at the top of the stairs.' After that, I accepted him as real and then became less aware of him, but felt he just popped in now again to see how we were doing; by this time, I knew he meant us no harm.

My happy married life continued and one day, we moved to Edinburgh with our jobs. We rented a top floor flat in a Georgian block. This was my fifth spirit encounter; I used to hear children laughing and playing when I was climbing the stairs, or sometimes when I opened my flat door. There were no children in the block; I had enquired a couple of times. It was as if I was hearing children playing and laughing from the past, caught in time. I did discover that years ago, the rooms we were in would have been the nursery rooms, before the house was converted. Again, the flat felt safe, and it was like hearing recordings of a distant past.

My further experiences were general feelings of uneasiness, sensing spirit, but not sure what it was. The sixth spirit experience that really struck me was after my sister-in-law died from smoking, which caused lung cancer. When she came to my house, she used to get up in the morning and start her day by having two cigarettes and a coffee to get going. For a few years on and off, I used to get a smell of cigarettes after she passed over, always in my hallway and lounge entrance. I used to open the front door or back door to see if the smell was elsewhere, but it never was. I always thought of her every time it happened and she has since come through in the readings I have had with other mediums.

By this time my awareness levels had changed, and I was very open to other people's energy. A quick example of this was when my father was dying. We were called because he had had a stroke and was given a few hours to live, so we rushed to his bedside. I knew his spirit was gone, but some small essence of something was holding him to the earth plane. 36 hours later, I asked the doctor why he had not passed yet, his breathing was so slight, stopping and starting; he just said the part of the brain for breathing was still intact. It suddenly came to me when I was on my own with him, that he did not want me to see him die; I can't tell you why or where this came from, I just knew. I said my good byes and told him to let go. My brothers understood, but stayed. He passed away a couple of hours later with my brothers at his side.

I have just realised reading back through this that I was shown a spirit, smelled a spirit, felt a spirit and heard them. Interesting how spirit works with us.

Well, onwards with my spirit journey. My life settled down again with just odd experiences, sensing presences from the spirit realm. My interest in angels, spirit, aliens and UFOs grew, and I fuelled this interest by reading books and watching documentaries on these subjects.

I had no idea at this point that my interest would be a basis for the next adventure on my spirit journey. This started around March 2010, when our advertising business moved out of the home to a local office space. I was delighted to discover we were in the unit next to a holistic healer. She was a crazy, wonderful lady, and was the second person I ever told about my experiences and what I felt about the worlds beyond ours, and she did not think I was crazy – YAY!

We got to know each other over cups of tea and one day I told her about a dream I'd had for years, and I felt I had lived it, but was not in this lifetime. In the dream, I would be visiting a black gravestone and vault, and also had glimpses of a large drawing room, a hall with lots of paintings and a bedroom I did not want to enter. She asked me if I'd do a past life regression with her and I nervously agreed. I discovered I'd lived in the early 1800s, in France. I was married and my husband died before I did, I believe he was in the military and died in a war. He was quite wealthy and we had a son and daughter, but I felt the daughter died young. I passed from what I said was scarlet fever in my late thirties. In the past life regression I visited my wedding scene, saw the drawing room and house, and also had a memory of taking my son away to school, and my husband's grave, which was the vault, and my death scene. In my death scene I was looking down at my own body. I had long brown hair and was in a white cotton nightdress. There was someone moving round my bed who I knew was a physician, and my son was standing looking over me; I had died. I now know the bedroom I did not want to enter was the bedroom I died in. This past life regression was a turning point for me in my mediumship and spirit interest.

Since then, I have had more past life regressions. One took me way back, to what I believe was the Viking era. I would be watching for boats on a cliff top for my husband to return. I believe my husband was a fisherman and one day his boat did not come home, and I know I spent a long time looking out to sea, waiting. I lived in a low stone crofter style cottage with a grass roof. Life was harsh, I passed when I was in my late fifties, looking a lot older than my years, and remember seeing on my death, my body floating out to sea as I was burnt. I remember relief that I was out of that harsh existence.

In my next past life experience, I was a young woman on a farm. I knew my mother had passed, and I had taken on the role of the main woman figure round the home. We had a large farmhouse kitchen with what I believe was a grey Lurcher sleeping by the fire. We had a water pump at the sink that you cranked up to pump water. Farm workers slept in the barn with the animals, and I also had younger siblings. My death was as a young woman, when there was a fire in the barn. I ran in to save lives and livestock when a beam fell on the left hand side of my body, and I was trapped. During this part of the regression, I got very hot and knew I did not die instantly. The one thing that stood out to me in this experience was that I was asked to then go on to my next life. This stunned me, as I saw myself as a female non-human form, not of earth, with long slender fingers and a flowing gown. I was looking out across a smooth surface that looked like a lake. In the sky there was a large planet with rings around it, and a smaller planet behind that one. It's at this point I realised we don't just reincarnate on earth, but on other planets as well.

My most recent past life regression took me back to about 400 ad; I was male, in my early twenties, and it felt as if I had lived in Greece, helping my merchant father run his business. We were well off; my father was ailing so I was making most of the decisions and was also married. I knew that I'd wanted to join my friends in what would have been an army role, but had to decide to stay at home and help the business.

A slight diversion there, but all part of the experience. Back to the cups of tea, and from one of the many conversations I had with my newfound holistic friend, she told me about Reiki healing, and that as a Reiki Master, she taught it. I was very drawn to this for spiritual reasons, and booked in to do my Reiki One Course. I was very excited, I was not too sure what to expect, but I also could not wait. Finally the day arrived, there were two of us on the course, and those two days changed my life. I realised, as I went through the day and was touched by spirit, that I had to forgive my adoptive mother and heal. After my attunement, I had the experience of seeing light beings in the room and auras round all three of us, I have never had that since, but know I will again one day. I now know these were my guides, showing themselves to me. This experience was amazing for me and opened me up to exploring further. I then joined a Reiki circle and a meditation circle, which alternated each week.

Something I should share with you is that when you start to change on your journey with spirit, it can affect your relationships with family and friends. You become excited, lifted and more positive, good things start to happen to you, and not everyone will be pleased about this. I sadly lost a friend of 18 years on my early journey. We would regularly meet up for a cup of tea. One day she asked me never to mention my circle, angels and new beliefs again. I then found out she had been messaging my husband saying I needed to see a psychologist. I was so upset and heartbroken at the time, and sadly it also affected my husband's friendship with her partner. But I now know that was her truth, not mine. I could have easily valued my friendship over spirit, but I knew by then my path was with them. I had to let go of the pain, and use my experiences to help others on the beginning of their light workers journey.

I continued with my Reiki journey and about ten months after doing my Reiki One, I did my Reiki two. This was still an awesome experience for me, but it was more about helping others heal through energy healing; I had cleared my pain and was ready to channel for spirit their healing divine energy.

I did not go on my Reiki journey ever thinking I'd practice and earn from it. I was one of those Reiki babies who felt I could not charge for this spirit gift they gave to others. I carried on in the circles, becoming more interested in mediumship. Then one day at the centre I attended a mediumship workshop. The morning was on a psychic level, but in the afternoon we took it in turns to connect to spirit clairvoyantly with the help of the medium, and bring in a loved one. My husband was there that day to support me on this new adventure, and he was surprised when I connected with his cousin and my mother. So was I! WOW I thought, and off we plodded home. What I had not realised in my lack of experience, is that I had been opened up like a beacon for spirit, but no help or advice for aftercare was given to me.

I started to hear voices in the house at night, see shadow figures, and at night, it felt as if spirit was queuing up in the bedroom to see me. My eldest son and one of their friends saw a young girl, and my eldest also saw someone in his bedroom. It was odd, as this new connection to spirit did not just affect me. (Quick flash-forward to today: my eldest son sees and hears spirit, it must run in the blood.) Any way, I went back to my Reiki

Master and she said I needed to shut down to them; she was not a medium but understood the importance of self-protection and taking control, so that is what I did. I asked in prayer for them to back off and leave me alone and they obliged. During this time, I learned that we all have a group of guides, and I know mine protected me when I asked for help.

One of the things my Reiki journey had done was make me look at my work life. I worked with my husband in our advertising business, but wanted to be more creative and work from home. I started to create a business making wedding guest books in my spare time. During this period I saw a medium for a reading at the holistic centre. I was amazed at this reading, with our relatives and friends popping in to say hello. He got my sons to a T, turned out the figure my eldest had been seeing in his bedroom was his grandfather, a guide to keep him on the straight and narrow, and he's still around him to this day. The medium had two messages for me. First, I was to continue with my creative path and second, spirit will be waiting for me to come back to mediumship when I felt ready. Well, I laughed at the latter, but hey, spirit knows your path, as my story will tell.

When my creative route took off, I created my business Youruniquescrapbook, which became a full time job, but I also drifted from my circles, and when the centre had to close, I did not look elsewhere to continue my spiritual path, as life was so busy at this time. I carried on with my life – reading about angels, UFOs and medium life stories, and watched all of those types of programmes on TV when I had a chance.

Then about three years ago, my husband's health took a turn for the worse; he had a bleed in his eye through high blood pressure and diabetes spiking. This affected his work and our income; also he felt down in himself; it was a tough period of time for us. During this time I felt unwell; I lived with fibromyalgia, so was used to experiencing dips in health. Eventually I took myself off to the doctor, to discover after tests and seeing a consultant that I had extremely high cholesterol and non-alcoholic liver disease. I was very overweight and unfit as well. It never ceases to amaze me, though, how your life's path works; through this ill health I joined a village gym to lose weight, and little did I know that this was the next part of my spiritual journey.

When I joined the gym, I met ladies I had not seen since my two lads were at primary school. There was one in particular whom I became friendly with; every time her I saw her I kept getting the word Reiki, Reiki, Reiki running through my head. I was reluctant to offer Reiki as I only had a small room and a chair, but the feeling would not go and one day I asked her if she would like some Reiki to help de-stress her, free of course. She jumped at the chance; through this, others started to hear about it and asked for Reiki too. I still could not get my head round charging for it but realised I would like to provide a holistic service. At this time, my interest in mediumship also soared again, but I knew I could not go back go to it without guidance and support.

I was drawn one day to see a medium called Berni, in my local area of Bristol. I loved her when I saw her on platform and emailed her afterwards to see if she taught or mentored people for mediumship. She kindly put me in touch with Maria from Heaven Sent Spiritualist Centre, where I went along one night to an open circle, and so the next stage of my journey really began.

My journey from when I joined Heaven Sent is a story in itself, so here it goes.

I had to laugh at spirit, as Heaven Sent is based in a horse stable with a converted barn, and I am allergic to horses! Mind you, I saw this as a sign I was in the right place, not as a bad sign. I sat in the medium development circle, attended occasional healing circles and workshops. I was dreaming of being a platform medium, but in March 2015 I attended a trance workshop, which changed this. It was an amazing day and I came away fascinated by trance. During the day we did mediation where I was introduced to my main guide, a monk called Harold, he had a writing feather in his hand and scrolls, and I felt he was encouraging me to write. We do inspiration writing as part of our development. As I'm dyslexic, I had in my head that I would struggle with this, but after this workshop, my writing started to develop. I realised in my early Reiki days I had been aware of a guide who was a monk, and it was Harold; I have to admit monks frighten me a bit, not sure why, but I now know there's nothing to be scared of, as Harold is so wise and patient with me.

By the end of 2014 I knew I wanted a holistic business, and in January 2015 I set up Bengalrose. Was I confident? No. I was scared and unsure but was being driven to do this; I doubted myself, feeling I was not experienced enough. But as with all jobs, you only gain experience from working and learning, so I offered free Reiki and readings for two months, to gain some work experience and build a reputation – and yes, I still had an issue with charging. What I learnt in these two months was that everything I did was with the intent of healing and creating wellbeing for my client. I realised my readings would bring about healing for them, and closure, and the Reiki also helped with healing and de-stressing them. I now knew this was my path and what I wanted to do in my life.

Around this time, my husband's health was still poor, and he was very down. I carried on with my holistic passion but was struggling, as I felt guilty doing something I loved while he was a bit lost in his life. Don't get me wrong, he supported me; it was my ego thinking this. In the early part of 2015 I attended a workshop called 'The Miracles of Life.' This workshop focuses on you shifting the blockage holding you back, and changing the way you think to create those miracles in life that you desire. Part of the day was spent writing a list of things you needed to release that were holding you back, and attaching names to them. We then burnt this to release them over to the universe. After I did mine I had an overwhelming rush of emotion as I realised the one thing that was holding me back was not on that paper, it was my husband. But was it my husband – or me? That was what I had to work out. I had realised that I was considering putting my holistic/mediumship journey on hold so I could help him find his path and be happier, but I did not want to stop my own spiritual journey.

Someone pointed out to me that day that sometimes you have to naturally shed those that hold you back, including loved ones when you are on a spiritual journey. Whoooo that shook me up, I loved this man, I wanted him to be happy and I wanted to be happy too. So I went home and put into practice what the workshop had taught me. Firstly, to imagine and feel you are living the future you want, which included my husband being well and in a job, feeling valued again. After a couple of weeks I decided to face him head on and took him out for a pub meal. I told him about what had happened at the workshop that he needed to start thinking positively to move on with his life. He admitted he was very down and he saw me soaring ahead, and he was being left behind. Something made me ask him, 'What is the one thing you really want to do?' and he said painting, and to be an artist. I asked him what was stopping him. He said he was afraid of failure. I know he realised at this point he was blocking his own path, and preventing himself from moving forward.

Not long after this I went on a mediumship retreat for two days. This was a dream; I had wanted to do one for ages. Yes, I had a pang of guilt, gallivanting off to enjoy myself, but I needed some space. The weekend was fab, I missed my home as I am a home bird, but the experience outweighed this. On the Saturday afternoon during a tea break, I checked my phone. There was a message from my husband; I clicked on it and my eyes popped – there was a painting of my dog. YES! He had done a painting! WOW! I cried, as it was awesome. He had gone through his own barrier, I spoke to him and I could hear a difference in his voice, I felt relief for him and for me as I knew this was a sign I could carry on with my light worker's journey not worrying about him, because he was back on his path. From these positive changes and way of thinking, he got a contract of work, which bought us financial security, and he carried on painting. A year later, he is still in this contract; he has had further health issues that have affected his eyes, but they are getting better and he's not down any more. His leap forward cleared the way for me to build my holistic business, as we were more secure financially.

When you take the spiritual path it will affect the world around you, especially in friendships and relationships. Don't fear this. As I have discovered, you shed the negativity and draw the positive and better people nearer to you. Also note, people do not go out of your life for good; they stay there as part of your everyday existence, but they are more in the background as you learn to protect yourself from the negative energy they bring. As with the story of my husband, you help others excel on their life's path without holding yourself back.

I have had a lot of people drift in and out of my life while on this spiritual journey, all for various reasons, all of them travelling their own journey and truth. I would place my experience of these people into three groups.

Group one: The Distant Group – This group is mainly friends who have pulled away and distanced themselves from me for various reasons that I will never know while on the earth plane. I have learnt not to seek answers, but to accept this is for the greater good in my life.

Group two: The Contemplators Group – This group is family and friends who accept you and the changes they see in you. They ask questions about spirit and quietly contemplate your answers; they will not be 100% believers yet, but you have let the sprit realm into their thoughts, which could be a start of their own spiritual journey.

Group three: The Accepters Group – these are family and friends that are intrigued and fully accept and understand you as you are. They know the messages and healing they receive are from a higher source. They are also ready to start on their spiritual path and embrace it.

So perhaps I should put into words my experiences across the three groups.

The Distant Group – I have already mentioned losing an old friend of 18 years which is a classic example, but I now know she was not ready to travel with me on my spiritual journey. In the last few years while at Heaven Sent I have lost couple of friends through their jealousy at my newfound happiness and enlightenment.

These people got involved in my journey, came to events, workshops I attended, but for some reason on their path they became resentful. This was their truth not mine, the lesson for me was not to hold malice against them, but send them love and light and hope they find happiness and learn to love themselves better. These, I learnt, are unhappy people lashing out at others, sometimes even from their subconscious.

The Contemplators Group – this group consists of some present friends and family members, but also people from my past being drawn to me. They might come to the odd event, workshop, and medium reading and healing. Their experiences are making them question their existence and path in life. They are experiencing things they do not understand, new feelings, and feeling and seeing spirit around them. They are excited by their new journey but also a bit doubtful and working to build their trust in what they are experiencing.

The Acceptors Group - these are the people in my life who have supported my journey, and been excited themselves by their own experiences, gained from workshops, events and messages. Some of them are taking their first steps with spirit, finding spiritualism, or perhaps working with spirit on the healing path. They might start taking their first steps on their Reiki journey. They might write their spirit journey one day, as I am – who knows? But the awesome thing is I have been a small part of their journey with my spirit team, as others have been of mine. We are all connected and our paths intertwine, nudging each other along our path with our spirit guides helping behind the scenes.

In my early days, I tried to steam ahead with my mediumship and light workers journey, and do everything I could for development. But I learnt to slow down my pace, trust and accept that it will flow as needed when it should. The one thing I did not understand is why my spiritual journey started in my late forties, and not in my teens or twenties, as I felt there was so much I could have done to help people. Well, I discovered recently that my life experience, good or bad, quite often relates to my clients. Spirit can show me my own past memories and experiences, to give evidence in readings, to help connect with people for healing messages and guidance from the spirit realm. I have also been told by spirit in readings that they have given me signs throughout my life, but I did not see them, or chose another path at the time, so they were trying to get me on board earlier, and that evidence is in this story.

Its quite magical how your guides work to guide you on your path. Here is a recent example:

I know from personal experience that spirit works in a magical way, planning behind the scenes to bring experiences for us to learn from and heal. This is one of those experiences that blew my mind; I don't know why I am always surprised at their magic, as by now I am well aware of it.

Well, I was on my second weekend retreat which involved working with spirit in workshops and as large groups over two days, and it was an awesome experience as always. On the Sunday morning I was awoken about 5.30 am, feeling very hot and uncomfortable, which was unusual for me. I heard a single birdsong from outside my window; I tried to get back to sleep but felt I needed some fresh air. I went to the kitchen area and to my surprise I was not alone – another early person was sitting outside. I joined her and we watched the sun start to creep over the horizon, and a gentle warm glow appeared in the morning sky. I sat there in the morning chill and watched the sun come up, the birdsong got louder and louder, and the peace of the world was broken as I watched a few clouds gently floating by. As I sat there I reflected on my spiritual journey, my self-doubt, my husband's health and being scared I would lose him, sending healing to him and my boys. My doubt about my spiritual journey came after a reading I gave, where one comment knocked me for six: *'I still believe, even after this reading.'* Poof - my ego fell in and I was lost. Looking back now as my light shines bright again, I brought through a few of her relatives and evidence, but she would not take any of it. I off-loaded this self-doubt at the retreat and our wonderful teacher reminded me that some people come to readings wanting to hear from one person, and block everything else. After this comment I trusted spirit again, as they never let you down.

After this time of reflection in the beauty of the morning sunrise with a cuppa and a chat, I went back to my room. My friend was in the shower so while waiting I was moved to do some inspiration writing. These words flowed in:

The magic of the sunrise

As the sun rises in the stillness of the morn

Mother Earth takes a breath of the divine

The light shining across the lands

Awaking all life old and to be born.

The silence is awakened by the light beams

The chorus of life sings out again to you

The stillness now has movement and a voice

Your heart is awakened to Mother Earth's tune.

As the sun rises into the protection of the earth

Your spirit stretches out to feel its warmth

Your body absorbs its life-giving energy

You find your path and life's worth.

As the sun sinks slowly below the horizon

The silence falls again on your spirit within

Know, my friends, you can hear our voice

In the silence there is love held frozen.

Sit in the silence and listen

Hear the night sound of the universe

Connect to the divine light beams

You will shine, sparkle and glisten.

I thought the words were very meaningful to my journey and thanked spirit. Well, it was not to end there. Later that morning I attended a workshop after an amazing trance session that left me elevated. The workshop was based around music; prior to coming, the teacher had a list of 44 songs and the names of the attendees, and asked spirit to pick us each a song. We would then listen to the song and words, reflecting on their meaning to us at that moment in time, revealing this to the group, and they would say what message they got from it for you as well. When it came to my turn and the song's first few lines were sung, I listened to the words and had a massive rise of emotion inside me, and I started sobbing. The song was called 'All things must pass' and here are some odd words from the song for you so you can see what I mean, to give you a feel of why it affected me. The song mentioned *sunrise, cloudbursts, love, don't give up, everything passes, moving on* and *facing another day*.

I have not written out the full words as I was not sure on copyright, but you can see from some of the words how it linked with my dawn experience. I had never heard the song before that day and it struck a chord with my spirit as I realised my experience early morning was all linked, and a message from the spirit realm. I realised all the fear I was holding inside had just been released, and I knew all would be OK.

The next day when I was at home, I got up early again and walked the dog as the sun came up. I played the song and felt inspired and at peace with the world around me. I realised that spirit had shown me their magical caring way of working with us, clearing any doubt I had a way, and giving me the healing I needed to move forward with my spiritual journey.

As I write this paragraph, I am two weeks on from this experience. The book content is flowing, but my spirit team told me they were struggling to work through me while I was trying to type on the computer; they wanted the information for the book to flow faster. They then suggested handwriting when they channelled the words, and it did come in quicker. But soon I realised they were giving me a lot of information on my dog walks, when I connected with my spirit team. I kept joking to them that I needed a note book on my walk because if I can't write it down, I forget it when I get home. I mentioned this to my husband and he said, 'Don't you have a voice memo on your phone?' I did not know this – how exciting! – so now I let them speak their words through me as I walk, talking into my phone, and I type it up later. It never ceases to amaze me how much they have to say!

My next experience of magic with the spirit realm was when they asked me to do a fairyologist course. This was gently introduced to me without me realising, when I got a sudden urge to make a fairy garden after seeing some other fairy gardens on social media. With my passion for gardening it was an exciting project, and I started seeing fairy objects everywhere. I created three fairy gardens, which have been greatly admired. Then the fairyologist course was presented to me through social media. I just knew I had to do it and was not sure why, as I had not really believed in fairies but had heard of elemental beings. It was an online course created by a world-renowned angel expert. I willingly completed the course as I really enjoyed it, but I did ask my spirit team why I had been led to it. They told me they wanted to write about the magic of the elemental beings and needed me to study, so they could use my mind to write about them from the spirit realm's perspective.

What I gained from the course, and the evidence I have seen since, is that fairies do exist. They have also made me more eco-friendly than I was before, for example picking up rubbish on my dog walks, especially plastic and metal. Because, you see, the elementals are here to look after Mother Earth and help heal her. I now want to guide others to their energies, as they can influence and change your life for the better. I have also been guided to have a fairy shop to help encourage others to make fairy gardens, and introduce them to the elementals.

After all this excitement and with the book still coming in, I wondered what would fill my time when the book was written, and how I could expand my holistic business with my newfound confidence in my mediumship. Well, they had already given me the sign 'Phone readings'. I had had two people I did not know contact me through social media, asking if I did them, but I felt unsure, as I really liked the physical contact at my readings and felt I would not deliver a good reading for them – ego strikes again. Spirit took heed of my thoughts and feelings and one day, someone I had met at a workshop but had moved away, contacted me to ask if would do a phone reading for her. This time, ego stood back a bit and I contacted one of my mentors, as I knew she did them. She was very supportive and told me to give it a go, and spirit would use the voice to connect. I went back to my acquaintance and said I would do it, but for free as it was my first one by phone. I held it in my healing room with the phone on loudspeaker, and trusted spirit. It was an awesome experience, lots of relatives, names, healing and guidance came through.

So a new arm of my business was born, thank you spirit.

While all of this has been going on in my life, my husband has had another health scare. This prompted us to decide to sell our house and go mortgage free, to take off the pressure and enjoy life more. I wrote out an affirmation to spirit; part of this was to ask for a short, stress-free chain; as I type this, yesterday we had an offer on the house, they have a first time buyer, and we have found a new house to buy that fits the criteria I asked for – 3- 4 bedroom house in a nice area, near dog walks, water and not too far from my children. I have been putting my trust out to spirit, as this move will affect those around me. We will be 25 minutes further away from my son's, but that's nothing in this world of ours, and I know it will all be fine.

Also during this last two weeks, I have had wonderful messages from spirit. I went to see a male medium on platform, he was wonderful, too. He bought my dad through, and after some great validation his message was about the move, that he was around helping in spirit, and all would be OK, and we would look back and know it was the best thing for us. He also said he saw a red sold sign on the board. Anyway, I told my estate agent this and her face dropped, as they had just changed their blue sold signs to red.

I was also honoured with a second message from my mother, and again, I got great validation that it was her; she then took the medium to near her death. At the time of her death I had not seen her for a long while; she had lung cancer that they believed had spread up from her ovaries, and she did not have long to live. I drove to see her in hospital, juggling a lot of unsaid emotions and words on the way. When I got to her bedside, I saw a frail, sick woman, a shadow of the former woman I had feared yet loved. I held her hand and our eyes met, words were not needed, and forgiveness was there. I left and never saw her again; she died a few days later. I had always wondered if she had understood and that all was OK. I got confirmation that night she had; I did not realise how much I needed this, and I was elevated. I thought I had healed these old wounds but I still needed this last message; but I also know that I was not ready to hear it until this point in my life.

I have mentioned the moving already; I had been asking spirit to guide and ensure all would be well with this move. As part of this life-changing event, we had to clear a big loft full of 18 years of stuff. Some of the items were from my husband's mum and dad's house, so my thoughts were with them as we cleared those out. I found one single old photo album up there, with pictures of a holiday they took in the late 1980s in Canada – it was great to see how healthy and well they were back then. Later on that day, we found some old video film; a couple of the clips were from that holiday. Then at the end of the day, hidden behind all the boxes, I found a box I did not recognise, and I realised it was from their house. There was not much in it, just a couple of crystal vases and an old pickle tray. I put the glass dishes in the pickle tray, and tipped it upside down to see if it was marked metal on the base, as I did this, a coin fell onto the counter. It was a Canadian dollar!

Wow – I did not see it when I examined the pickle dish, and I realised I had had three signs from them telling me all's ok. The way spirit works always surprises me; I should be used to it by now, but I think I will always be in awe of them.

Well, to conclude my journey with spirit for this book, I love working with spirit. As well as being a clairvoyant medium, I now sit in a trance closed circle, also we have started touching on the physical mediumship which has been an amazing journey so far in it self. The trance opened me up to channelling writing from spirit to spread their love and wisdom. The trance has also changed my healing energies within my healing work for the better. I have also recently been made aware that I have an Alien guide, tall grey being that I have drawn for all to see if they wish to.

My own words of wisdom for you are TRUST. Trust your own first instincts and intuition as you walk your earth's path and don't let your ego rule your head. Spirit is truly magical in the way it seeks to help mankind. I am just a very, very tiny part of this, but I know everything we do in the love and light helps them make a step forward in guiding us to what we could be. We could be awesome beings, living on a nurtured, clean planet, helping and guiding each other to be the best we can be. No jealousy or resentment, just love, kindness, and the divine light of trust.

These words have been in my head this week since I watched the medium at work that gave my parents' messages. Something just clicked inside: *"I am a spiritual being experiencing a life on earth, I walk in human form, taking human steps and experiencing the physical plane, learning, and collecting knowledge and wisdom on the way. I am happy and at peace with my temporary form. Love and blessings."*

Chapter 4

Magic of the Elementals

We would like to just touch on this subject and make you aware of elemental beings that live amongst you on a metaphysical level on your earth. A lot of you would say this is make believe, a fairy tale, but my friends, if you believe in the spirit world, the afterlife, aliens, and the existence of other planets, dimensions and realms, then why is there not an elemental world? The fairies, pixies, goblins, mermaids and unicorns are the main recognised elemental beings in your world. There are many books on earth about the elementals for you to research; here, we will just give you a brief glimpse into their world.

Back in your time 1493, a man called Paracelsus was born. He became a philosopher, physician, botanist and astrologer; he had great connection with spirit and the universe around him. He had great insight into the elemental beings, and understood them, and the role that elemental spirits played in nature. He came to the conclusion that it was intelligences other than those possessed by human beings that justified his understanding of natural phenomenon on Mother Earth. Paracelsus knew that the visible world was a secondary phenomenon. The invisible part of the world is more important, and can only be discovered through the light of Nature. In his book the Paramirum, he writes: *"We men on earth, what do we know about phenomena without the light of Nature? It is the light of Nature that makes invisible things visible."* This man was given the gift of great understanding and seeing beyond the 3D physical existence. He was ahead of his time, he knew that air, earth, fire and water were key to Mother Nature's existence and there were unseen forces helping her. He was clever enough to never declare he had seen these beings; he wrote in a mythical way, as he was living in an era of strong church beliefs and dark times. Please read his works, as you will learn a lot from them, my friends.

These beings are vital to your earth's existence; they cleanse, purify and help protect Mother Earth. Elemental beings live in one of the energy planes in your earth energy fields. They are just a touch away from you – they can be sitting on your shoulder, or next to you in a flower border. A lot of mankind will be unaware of this, as they are of the spirit realm, but their existence is real, my friends.

We do see some of you doubt the existence of fairies and elemental beings that can live on earth as part of Earth's existence. They are portrayed in your world's folklore, going back centuries in many cultures, and like the glimpses of the spirit realm, there have also been glimpses of elemental beings too.

Elemental beings were on the earth plane in a 3-4D existence when they lived among man many centuries ago. But they raised themselves up into a higher plane of energy – the metaphysical level – to survive. It is as if they pulled a magical cloak over themselves as protection against mankind's naivety and fear about any beings different to mankind. Your earth has what we call energy planes – they are not realms or dimensions. These run alongside your existence; imagine that as you walk through the air you breathe, you walk through their world too. We hope this makes sense to you my friends, because trying to explain the different layers of existence around earth is hard, as there are not many earth words that can help us with this. You will see for yourself one day, when you return to us with understanding of how the earth works.

The elementals are based round air, earth, fire and water; this is because they are protecting every element of your planet. For Mother Earth to be at her best, these elements need to be in balance, just as they need to be in the physical human being. Mankind has been made aware of this through us channelling this information to you, and it is important, my friends that you try to understand why the elemental beings are here on your earth.

The main elemental we are going to talk about first is the fairies, because they work with Mother Nature very closely, especially plants. There are various sets of fairy beings around the world that exist within their own communities; they have families, royalty and social hierarchy with their own cultures. The best way we can explain this is that they have lived a physical existence on earth, with an ego, in an earth plane veiled from mankind for their protection.

The fairies and other elementals are very choosy about who they let see them. The reason for this, my friends, is because as you can imagine, they are very protective of their existence, and their importance is so key to Mother Earth and her survival. They are battling against the pollution that mankind has made, and with the shift of energy on the earth in the last few years, a lot of you are becoming more aware of elementals and their role within Earth's make up.

The main reason we wanted to talk about the fairies is because they are very eco- friendly beings and they want every human to be that way too. The word Fairyologist has been created for mankind; for those of you who are drawn to spirit, healing, readings and that way of being, might be drawn to train to be a fairyologist. This training makes you aware of the elementals; giving you understanding so you can teach it to others.

This is a wonderful thing for this to happen, my friends, and as you are aware, our friend who helps us channel this book is now a fairyologist. The changes this way of seeing has made for her are that she is becoming more eco- friendly; on her dog walks she now picks up the rubbish she sees, and she has also stepped up home recycling. We have also seen her awareness alter regarding what she puts on her garden and plants to control slugs and disease, and in the house detergents she chooses.

Becoming a non-meat eater is something the elementals also encourage you to do. The natural killing for human survival was acceptable in the past, as mankind would give thanks to the spirit of the animal when it was gifted for food. But now, the elementals are upset by mass farming, and they want to express that to you. Imagine the stress and fear those animals experience, which is absorbed into their energy and body, which you then eat, absorbing the negative energy in the meat. Something to think about, is it not?

This experience has made our friend look at the world around her in a different way. She is not making all the changes that the elementals would like her to make, but we understand this is a gradual process, because it takes a lot for a human to break the habits of a lifetime. For those of you that choose to become a fairyologist, you will be embracing the elementals by changing your lifestyle, and spreading their words out to mankind.

A lot of elementals stay hidden for their safety, but with your digital cameras, you can now capture them, just like you can capture the orbs of spirit, if they choose to show themselves to you. The fairies will show up as a small, blurred smudge, the shape of a gingerbread man with a glow or tiny white orbs that flutter from side to side like fireflies. When you do a Fairyologist course and get the urge to take a picture of a wild area or woods, study the picture when you get home; sometimes you might see the shape of a fairy between the leaves, or a face in the gaps. Other elementals like the pixies will show themselves too, as faces on leaves or in the gaps between the leaves. These signs we have described are the energies of the elemental, and show they are there with you. Some of you know how hard it is to capture spirit on film and video, and elementals are the same.

Elementals have been known to choose to take on a physical earth form existence, as we do in the spirit world, so they can carry out a specific purpose. Do you know any humans that are very petite, angelic looking, or redheads with passion and a temper, or great swimmers who love the water and are keen to look after the environment? These are most likely elementals, reincarnated to help the earth at this time.

Still questioning why there cannot be a place where fairies, goblins, pixies, mermaids and unicorns exist? Where do you think this has all come from? Look back centuries into your mythical beliefs, as these are not ideas from modern times, but go back a long way. As with angels and spirit, humans have glimpsed these light beings, by being fortunate enough to be in the right state of mind where they see them and can experience them. People who do believe think these beings have a mischievous quality, but they are very much like most of you – they only want the best for your world, but have a fun, loving existence while trying to achieve it. So learn to connect to them as you do the spirit realm, and the elementals will help guide you on how to be a better human, how to love all your world's nature and animal kingdom, and your earth's environment. So, my friends think about it and reflect on what we have to say about the elemental world that surrounds you and is knocking on your door.

Who are the elementals?

The elemental plane watches over the air, earth, fire and water elements of your earth. Within each of the four elements are nature spirits – the spiritual essence of that element. They exist in an etheric form of flesh, blood and bones. Let us explain what 'etheric' means. Think of the human aura; this is your etheric body. Without going into too much science, it is an energy field made out of different matter. The Etheric Body gives vitality, health, life and organisation to the Physical Body. It attunes your consciousness to the principle of energy. It draws energies from the higher bodies down into our physical consciousness, and it gives you awareness of types of subtle energy in the physical body and your environment. We know that those of you on the spiritual healing and mediumship path will already be aware of this. Earth people relate this etheric form to heaven and the angels, which are etheric forms that think with no ego, created from the thoughts of divine source, your God.

Elementals do have etheric bodies with bones and flesh, and they have the ego too. They cannot be destroyed by the earth's material elements such as fire, air, earth, and water because they are etheric in nature. They can live a long time, as many as 300-1000 of your years; they live lives as you do, have families, eat, drink, talk, play and sleep.

Air elementals

Sylphs - they are the air fairies, tiny beings with wings, and their magic lies in bringing healing to our air and sky. They help with airflow and atmospheric conditions around Mother Earth, and purification of the air; they also work on the mental plane in the earth's atmosphere where the negative mental thoughts collect. This is vital work for us in the spirit realm, as when there's lots of negative energy, we can have trouble penetrating it. Sylphs like to hang out on hills and mountaintops where they can be close to the sky. You can call upon them at any time to clear polluted air around you, and you will notice a difference.

Earth elementals

Gnomes - these sweet tempered, helpful beings are dwarf in size; the males are often seen with long beards. These small beings are Earth dwellers living inside the earth, and their job is to tend to the four seasons. They process the waste and by-products that are an inevitable part of our everyday existence, and purge the earth of poisons and pollutants that are dangerous to the physical bodies of mankind, animal and plant life. They also protect the earth's lay lines and undergrowth. Their behaviour can be mischievous, and like all elementals, they like to have fun.

Brownies - it is believed in your folklore that each house has its own brownie; they are good-natured, small creatures with tanned skins, which dress in brown. They like to perform helpful services; ask your brownie to help you keep your house clean and see what happens.

Leprechauns - these ancient spirits are based in Ireland, and were once earth dwellers; but as with all elementals, they decided to shift into a higher vibration, but remain on earth living amongst us. They seldom show themselves but when they do, they appear green and show ages of wisdom in their faces – and love to have fun.

Elves - are secretive beings that guard the trees. Elves tend to the roots of trees and plants, and are of vital importance to the soil ecosystems of your planet. Elves love the rain, as it is the best thing to energetically purify the undergrowth of which they are the guardians. They help rebalance the world we live in, as do all elementals. They are waiting for you to connect with them, to reawaken the knowledge you have within you about themselves, pixies and their purpose.

Pixies - they are a small people, smaller that elves, related mostly to the Celtic folklore of your world. You have heard of magical pixie dust? The dust comes from the time they mined, gold, jewels and crystals; the dust the mining created was magical to them. They practise a magic that can help you, they are not too mischievous, and quieter in nature than some elementals.

Rock people - Your earth stones and crystals are from the mineral kingdom, and they each have their own life force, which has lived on earth since it was formed. The rock people are keepers of the rocks with spirit within; look carefully and you can see their faces and different personalities in the rocks. Your individual earth crystals all have their own special purpose and vibration, especially for healing and protection. They can also store great amounts of information, and absorb earth messages and history. Tune into your earth's rocks and crystals to hear what messages they have for you.

Fire elementals

Salamanders – their story is written in your ancient folklore; they inhabit the element of fire, and some have been seen in human form or as an animal - usually a lizard. The lizards live within the wood in the forests, and this protects them when there is a forest fire. So they have seemed like magic to a lot of your ancient cultures, as they have survived forest fires by curling up in the trees themselves for protection. They create the landscape of reality on earth and mainly inhabit forests, mountains and fires; lighting, light and fire orbs are often seen when they are near. A very powerful elemental in their world.

Djin – are also fire elementals that are believed to help you; they can make a wish for you, as well as grant wishes to help those they believe in. They are found more in the Islamic states, and they have free will as you do. In ancient times, they were thought to be a devilish creature, but they were misinterpreted, as they chose whom they helped. They are also the basis for the Genies in the lamp stories of ancient times.

Water elementals

Sea-sprites - they are tiny wingless beings that live in water and love playing in the sea spray in the surf. **Undines** are similar to sea-sprites, but are more in the water than the sea spray. They are silvery, reflecting the sunlight, darting about in the water or waves. They help to cleanse the water in the sun and moonlight.

Nymphs – these are beautiful female nature fairies that oversee the waters of your world. Their legends go as far back as the ancient Greeks, who viewed them as minor goddesses and saw them as beautiful female creatures of mystery.

Mermaids – Mermaids and Mermen are water dwelling, living in the oceans, rivers and lakes, and are part of the elemental kingdom protecting the environment. They show up in ancient cultures of the world, even before Christianity came to earth. They are well known on earth as Merpeople, recognised by their fish tails and human top form. There are also Mer-fairies with a fish tale, human form and wings, but of a smaller build; they are the caretakers of freshwaters like lakes, rivers and streams.

These also reside near land in the seas; as with all elemental beings, there are different mermaids and cultures in the Mer-world.

Tree spirits

Trees are such a powerful element of your earth, and the passionate tree fairies love their trees. The tree fairies live amongst the trees to protect them and benefit from them. Every tree has a spirit, sometimes called a tree person. They do show themselves; take a look at the trees around you and you will see a face, each with its own character. They are part of the tree and absorb all that goes on around it with the seasons of Mother Earth. There is a third elemental connected with the trees, commonly known as the Green Man or Jack in the Green, which has emerged from the Celtic and Gaelic Spiritual beliefs. The Green Man is a deity that watches over the trees, supporting death and rebirth amongst them. Your past pagan tribes would worship the Green Man and the trees, the trees bringing great wisdom, strength and knowledge to their worship and lives.

We love to see humans embrace your trees, hugging them and asking them for their healing and wisdom. We asked our human friend to do this for us, and this is the message she got back from the tree:

"We have been here a long time, my friend, cleansing your earth, helping Mother Earth stay pure, and trying to keep the memories of that first divine spark of existence for us. As we grow, die back and re-grow, we adapt to the world around us and the pollutants mankind have made. So we ask you, my friend, to assist us and help cleanse the environment in your world. The small changes will make a big difference; we know you are becoming more aware and we thank you for this."

As well as giving great spiritual healing, the physical properties of trees can give healing. Think of the willow that was a base for your original aspirin, and a flexible, unbreakable branch, which was symbolic in ancient times on earth.

Unicorns

These beautiful, solitary, free spirit, single-horned horses have been portrayed in your art across your world in different cultures, way back to the ancient times. They are very pure spirited animals, and children especially connect to their energy. When they lived on the physical earth plane they were hunted for their horns and the magic they could provide, so like all the elementals, they lifted themselves up to the metaphysical level. Only people with pure hearts can see them, and they will be attracted to them all their lives. If you work with spirit, ask them to show your unicorn to you; if you have one as part of your spirit team, it will show itself. They are protective companions, connecting with your pure inner child, and will bring fun to your way of being.

The magical conclusion

You will draw your own conclusions, my friends, on your beliefs, from everything written in this book. We have just touched on the Elementals, as we wanted to make you aware of these unseen forces that help your planet every day. If you have managed to elevate yourself to a higher spiritual vibration, you will be able to connect and if lucky, you will see them, too.

They are very protective of both your earth and themselves. They were seen a long time ago as a threat to humans living in their restricted religious beliefs, and the elementals and their magical powers were seen as evil, and a threat to their own power. So the elementals all raised themselves to a higher vibration to carry on their wonderful work. They will connect with those of pure of heart, but you have to prove yourselves to them before you will receive their loyalty.

If you wish to connect with them, my friends, go out into nature and respect it, sit in the wood and send out your thoughts. They will hear you; the signs might be a rustle nearby, or you may see something quick in your peripheral vision or small flashes of light; stay tuned in, as these are ways they can show themselves. Once you are aware of them, ask them how you can help them. Then, build your relationship with them by carrying out their instructions – which will all be ways to benefit Mother Earth by helping her to purify and cleanse herself of pollutants.

Enjoy your journey with your elemental friends. We will be watching your progress.

Chapter 5

The Magical Spirit Alphabet

We wanted to give you a gift of our wisdom and thought it would be fun to use your western alphabet as a structured guidance tool. These are words you can adapt for your spiritual church services and circles so you can teach and guide others with them.

Have you ever thought about your world and the world you live in? Do you ever pause and look around you and wonder at the miracle of life and the magic of creation? Do you ever look beyond your own needs, look at others, look deep inside them, ask what drives those people, and what makes them who they are today?

What are we saying, my friends, is that you need to look beyond yourself, look at those around you, and understand their inner feelings, what makes them tick, what are their beliefs, why do they believe what they do? Think about what their history might be, and what their belief system is based on. A lot of these belief systems go back thousands of years, so they can't be dismissed out of hand, my friends. All belief systems have had the spark of the Divine at some point, which has led to the religions they are today.

Some of you see a fat person, a skinny person, or a handicapped person, and you judge them, my friends. For example, you might question why the fat person cannot lose weight. Quite often, the reason for being different is lying under the skin, which cannot be seen by the human eye. Also, my friends, this person could be very unhappy, or have an underlying illness that causes them to be overweight. You know you need to not judge, but find out about that person, talk to them, make them a friend; it might be that friendship is what changes their lives, so use your third eye to see beyond the physical form to truly understand a fellow human being.

Try and look beyond your own needs, but as we say this, my friends, remember that your own needs must also be met. You need to find happiness and contentment in your life, and when you are that happy and content person, you will shine out, and you will be able to look at others and try to understand them, and not judge any more.

Take these words with you and spread these thoughts, and if you see someone judging, be brave; ask them to stand back and ask why are they judging, why are they laughing at or criticising that person? Who are they? What right do they have? What right do you have, my friends? You have the right to be kind and loving. Remember, you are pure spirit within, and that pure spirit will curl up inside and try to avoid every bad thought or judgment that you make that is not good and kind to others. Your spirit does not wish to do this; your spirit wishes to shine out my friends, shine out to mankind and help mankind move forward in love and light.

So, my friends, don't judge today, listen, befriend, be kind and loving and see how your world changes around you for the better. The challenge when you come down to earth is that your memory of your spirit realm is not connected to your earth memory. Your inner spirit and higher self still contains this information for you to tap into. As you have grown in your human form, we ask you to place on your path's journey your aim – to find the love and light, to recognise the Divine light, to live your life in a good wholesome way, and give love to others. One of the main keys of being successful in this, is being well in yourself, looking after yourself, and finding true inner peace.

As the spirit grows in the baby, who is the human host, and the essence of the human form, you start the life path that was chosen for you. On this path there are different forks that you can take; these paths will take you on a different route. Your free will, choice and ego will help you decide which path to take, which will sometimes mean slightly veering off your rightful life's path. Remember we are always there, trying to keep you on your rightful path all the time, but on your journey in life you cannot always stay exactly on course, because other factors come in. Other people's journeys will affect you, because although we try to plan millions of lives at once, as you can imagine, my friends, there are always going to be a few hiccups that come in the course of all your lives. But keep the Faith, and have the TRUST that whatever path you go off on, we will try our best to steer you back to the correct path.

The memory of your spirit life and your new journey's path on earth is always held within your inner spirit; your spirit will always be searching for the divine experience on your life's journey. Now it might be that in a previous life on Earth, you did not reach this goal you set yourself, so you have come back to find spirit and help others. It might be you have returned and are a teacher, a nurse, a carer, giving, caring for others, not taking much back; that is you finding your path to the light, my friends. Remember, finding the light is not always finding religion, spiritualism, or being a medium or healer, it can be as simple as being a mother or a father, raising your children in a loving, kind, understanding environment. Each individual will have their own lessons to learn, never to be compared to another's, and all for the greater good, as this is the intention set for their life path.

For those of you that are inquisitive, and wondering what is out there beyond your own human needs, there is so much that can be offered to you, my friends. You all seek the magical moment when you realise spirit realm is real, and you are touched by spirit. When this happens, you will feel lighter, you might weep tears of joy; a lot of fears will be released and you will be excited to explore more and find out more about us. There is great excitement for us when we see you achieve this – we all sit there wishing and waiting for this moment to happen to you. But our time is not the same as yours my friends; there is no rush in our realm. You can come back home and try again, we evaluate, look at your life, and think about what we can do to help you with your ascension in the spirit realm, and to bring you towards the all-knowing light and Divine wisdom of God, from the Divine source. Though this is the purpose of your journey, some ask, why don't we have that from the moment we open our eyes? Why can't we know about everything, and have that light, so we can help each other from the moment we are born? You don't have everything at once, because the challenge for you in the spirit realm is to discover what you have here in the spirit realm on your chosen journey on earth – on a planet or other place you choose to be part of, remember this is how mankind will ascend. In the spirit realm, you know the divine pure love exists, because you live every moment with that love light pure source. When you go to the physical human form on earth, or wherever it is you chose to go, my friends, the chosen body and mind does not know about the spirit realm and that is what you have to discover together, for mankind or other species out there.

Enjoy your journey, my friends; the fact you are reading this book is bringing you further on your path, and we look forward to seeing you develop and are waiting, smiling down on you as you progress on your journey.

Now read the spiritual alphabet, learn from its magical earth words, the words of spirit and wisdom. These words have been written with the intent that you share your teachings and moments of philosophy amongst yourselves. Speaking our words will bring guidance, healing and expansion of thought for the spiritual realm amongst your friends and congregations in the spirit churches and circles.

Ascension

We hear a lot of you ask about ascension – you wonder what it is, and what it means to you, mankind and the spirit realm. We realise there are a lot of books on the earth plane that explain about ascension, which have been channelled from spirit, but they are quite in depth and complicated, and not everybody can absorb such information. So we thought we would take this opportunity to do a simple breakdown of what ascension is. Ascension is a word that was given to mankind to describe the spirit realm, its various spirit forms and levels of development. You are already aware of the high archangels and God, who is our high being of divine light; they are pure spirit, they have not been to other planets, realms or other dimensions to live in a physical form, and they are pure love. We suppose the word that could be used is they have not been *tainted*, they have not been affected by a life that has not been lived in pure love, and they ascend in the higher levels of the spirit realm to the highest point they can.

As we have said in the book 'Utopia', we have sixty-five levels of ascension, to put it into mathematical form for you, but we did not go into depth regarding what there actually is within those sixty-five levels, which is more levels. As you can imagine, explaining these levels can be quite complicated. Basically, you have your guides that come to you and work with you, and healers; some of those from the spirit realm have lived lives on earth or in other places. While living these lives, they absorb some of the qualities and take on the essence of that being they were. Yes, we do ascend, we do work our way up, but there is a certain point where we will stop our ascension because we are not of pure love and light energy any more, because we have taken on the essence of another physical being, knowledge and wisdom from other places. The pure love and light beings in the higher realms take on this knowledge as well, but they have not actually lived in a physical body, which would have affected their pure spirit. So we hope this simple explanation is clear to you, my friends.

We see amongst some of the light workers on earth that they are trying to ascend, by blocking out your daily news, your daily world around you, to try and reach that ascension that a human form desires. At the moment, you are working in what we have called a 3D dimension, where you are interacting with each other, creating wars and darkness. But there are those amongst you that are trying to stop these events, and it's like a tug of war for you. Some members of mankind are trying to ascend out of this tug of war at the moment, with the help of the spirit realm and other species beyond earth.

You are ascending into the 4D dimension, my friends, and many light workers are recognising this. But what you have to realise is that this generation is not going to ascend to much beyond where it is at the moment, because you are the workers, my friends, you are the generation that is laying the foundations for the next generation, which will ascend into the 4th Dimension and change the way mankind thinks. Then, because of the way mankind works, with your ego and free will, that generation could be looking at a couple more generations before humans are actually heading towards a pure way of being in the fifth dimension of living, in a pure love, positive way, with no unnecessary harm to other humans or animals on your world.

As you ascend, you will explore your galaxy and universe, tapping into the knowledge pot and the wisdom that lies out there waiting for you. So you see, my friends, we paint this picture of ascension so you can understand what mankind can achieve. But what we want you to understand at the moment is that yes, live the most honest pure life you can helping others, guiding, teaching this to others, especially your children. But you should also learn to protect yourselves from the fear and the anger in the world, because it is you that needs to help these areas, and if you take on that fear and anger you will not be able to progress like us, my friends.

So you need to be aware of what's going on around you, and what needs changing. We know your news agencies and your governments filter what they want you to see and hear, and there is stuff hidden from you. In the Western world, which is supposed to uphold free speech and thinking, you are still being dictated to, my friends; you are not as free as you think, either in your way of thinking, or of finding out truthful information. This is another area we need you to work on, to make all humans honest in bringing all information out on the table so that all of mankind can see it, evaluate it, and make their decision on where they want to be in their world in the universe. In the Eastern parts of your world there are countries with dictatorships that are holding the earth back. They do have their Buddha and their religious beliefs where they are capable of reaching an ascension state, but they are quite separated from the main part of their Eastern countries. They do their best to spread their religious beliefs, which helps man, but due to their dictatorships, they are behind with all this compared to the Western world.

So I suppose what we are saying is that we are focusing more on the Western world at the moment, as they have more freethinking and you can make changes that are needed quicker for the spirit realm, as the shift occurs on earth. We will also be plugging away at the Eastern world, hoping as the Western world shifts and ascends, the Eastern countries will open up and see the light, all merging and working together and helping each other. We look forward to mankind's ascension at a steady, safe pace, for the good of all.

Believe

The word believe, my friends, is another word we find quite magical in your world. It's a word used by many of you many a times a day. Our question concerns the word 'believe', and what meaning it has for you. We are interested in the use of the word as in, do you believe? I believe in... What do you believe in? If only we all believed in...

Believe is a word you use in your language to show you have strong conviction and faith in something. You can believe in a person, believe they can get through an illness, or break their addiction. You can believe in religion, spiritualism, whatever it is that's been put in your path at that time for you to consider and believe in. Part of this believing is finding trust and faith.

But the main thing we want you to consider, my friends, is: Do you believe in yourself? To make your journey on earth the best it can be, you must achieve self-belief, and know what you desire to achieve. We have already talked about thoughts, positive thinking and affirmations; all of this is easy to say, and the words can spill out of you, but if you do not have that belief in yourself and the world around you, your hopes will not come to fruition. To have faith in your world and the spiritual realm, you need this self-belief, or you will never fully achieve what you have planned in this earth's lifetime.

Look at your young children as they innocently play; their belief system has not yet quite developed. They do not have these thoughts, or the world on their shoulders; they will perhaps be observing their parents worshiping in the different religions around your world, and they are being shown their parents' beliefs, which the adults want them to follow.

Of course, many of you do take on your cultural beliefs, and believe them to be right – remember, a lot of your cultural beliefs are based on the divine spirit, and something sparked that belief in ancient times. It is quite interesting to us that you do have these different cultural religions and belief systems around your world. We know that many of them come back to the core, the source of the light; it is just shown in different ways, in the textbook words and images and in the way they worship.

71

As children grow, some of them will have the character and strength to challenge the cultural belief system they have been indoctrinated with – remember the Star Children. This is always very interesting to us, my friends, as this gives us an opportunity to place in front of them the truth that's out there, and the way they can live their lives towards the love and light. We show them a career that will bring positivity and love to other people's lives, for example, medical roles, carers, teachers and healers, in the hope they follow the right path for them.

When you take on a task in your daily lives, it can be anything from decorating a room, doing the washing, cooking, painting, taking tests and exams, and we see that many of you get discouraged quickly if the task goes wrong. This is because you have not believed you can do your best at this task and all will be OK. If there is a moment when things are not going quite right, just stop, walk away from the wet paint, walk away from whatever the issue is within your life that's causing you to feel discouraged. Just take that pause, take a deep breath, and think: 'I do believe, I trust, I can do this.' Ask your spirit guides to help you, and you will find you will move forward with a new energy – and all *will* be OK!

Another example is when you are doing exams, and feel you are struggling because you have to achieve that high percentage to get to where you need to be. Don't worry about the failure side of the situation, my friends, because that is what you will create for yourself. Look at the positive side and imagine yourself succeeding, that you have got that percentage you need, and you have what you need in your life to move forward; in other words, believe in yourself.

Then there is the other side of the coin to consider, if you are held back and don't quite achieve your goal the first time. We would like to say to you, my friends, just to make you think about it, that it is not always because of your belief system. Sometimes – and we are not being mischievous when we do this – we like to see you stretch yourselves and think a bit more about life. Perhaps you were not quite ready. A good example is a learner driver in your world; they fail their first test, and there's no reason why they should have failed as they had an excellent teacher and drove well. But they were stopped in their progress, as in their head, they were going to drive fast, get their mates in the car and show off. You would be unaware of their thinking, but the spirit realm knows all, and perhaps we took the decision to slow that person down for their own safety, or the safety of another, to make them realise. You do have to sometimes work harder to achieve what you want in your lives.

So yes, on one hand we are saying believe in yourself, have faith and try your best, and on the other hand, sometimes your lessons are not to succeed all the time. If you do have a little failure, don't see it as a downer, see it as a positive thought. Think, 'OK, why did this happen to me? Perhaps I need to slow down; perhaps I am not quite ready. I will try again and I know I will succeed next time.' Remember, my friends, all of this will strengthen your character for your life's challenges.

It's just having that belief and faith that, whatever happens to you in your life and your life's journey, is for a reason. You are not being sent things to upset you when you do have a failure; that is not what we want to achieve, as we live in pure love and spirit and laughter, my friends. We want you all to be happy, but sometimes it's just the lesson that needs to be learnt at that moment in time.

So, my friends believe in yourself and also believe in others around you. Have faith in your fellow man. If you feel disillusioned by one person, take a look around, as there is going to be someone else that will bring positivity back and wipe out that disillusioned feeling for you, and this will give you back the faith you need.

If your life is not how you want it to be, you have to make the changes, my friends. You have to believe you can, and put things into action for this to happen. Lay out a plan, take a step at a time, and believe you will achieve it.

We hope this has helped you, my friends, to believe in yourself, and believe in your journey while here on earth. Whatever happens is for a reason, just TRUST and have faith in yourself and us.

Consideration

Consideration is a word created by mankind that we like, because it is a word that makes you think about yourself and other people around you. Now, thinking about yourself is key, giving consideration to how you are in your own wellbeing, your mental state and your spirituality – this is all part of your path on Earth. Consideration of yourself is very important, you must not feel selfish putting yourself first most of the time, my friends, because it is important you are at your best to achieve your life's path. When you are at your best in both health and in spirit, you can give your best to those around you in your lives. And if you work on the spiritual path as a medium or a healer, it is very important you stay very, very healthy and mentally balanced, my friends, as this work uses a lot of your energy.

So why do we want to talk about consideration and reflect on it with you? Please consider that consideration is something you should give to everybody around you, including members of the animal kingdom. A lot of mankind is not considerate to others and they think about themselves a lot. Now, as we said earlier, thinking about yourselves in the right ways is good, but many people put themselves way above others with no consideration of them, and this affects other people's lives. They put themselves first in gathering their food, health and wealth, and this affects their spiritual path, as they don't see the light. Now, the balance for you and mankind is to make sure you consider yourself in a pure love and light way, so you are spiritually, healthy and mentally well, you have enough food and wealth to become comfortable, but you also consider others around you; this is what we would like to achieve for mankind.

So on a daily basis, you need to consider those around you, step back and take a look and think, are they OK, or do they need an extra hand with something? Do you have an old relative that you have not spoken to for a while? Perhaps just picking up the phone to speak to them will make a difference to their day, and that's consideration, my friends. It only takes a few of your minutes out of your day to achieve this, to help others on a regular basis – any small, kind act like this makes such a difference to other people.

You know, when we look at the word consideration for you, we see you using it without you realising it, with every decision you make on your life's journey. It's as simple as which shop to shop in, restaurant to eat in, which path to take on a walk, which holiday to book, all these options you have to consider my friends, all make an impact on your life and the path you take; remember, no meeting is by chance, all choices and people you meet are part of your journey. We are always in the background; some of you are aware of this, some not, as we try to direct you on the path that might change things for you. For example, that holiday choice might lead you to meet someone that could change your life on your spiritual path, love or work life, and we try to steer you in the direction you need to go in.

But as we have said before, you can imagine it is very hard to get you exactly on that path, because the challenge for us with mankind and the spirit that links with you is the human free will, and we do enjoy this part of the challenge with you.

So think, my friends, when you get up in the morning you consider which vessel you will drink out of, you consider what you are going to wear, you consider what the weather is going to be that day, or whether to watch the news or the last episode of a soap opera you missed. There are hundreds of things you consider, every moment of every day in your lives.

So why not consider other people more, why not consider the world around you, why not take action to help and promote areas of your world that need help? Join a charity, be the leader of a charity, try jumping out of your comfort zone and consider the world around you more, my friends. You will be surprised on how your world will change, your self will change and the people around you will change. Everything will become better and stronger and you will be happier, and more love and light will shine into your immediate world and existence.

But may I add to this is that you are so important, my friends. You are unique, each of you is an individual and that is what we love about you and mankind, that each one of you has your own spark, your own divine wisdom and your own spirit. The great thing is that when the spirit blends with its chosen body, what a wonderful being you become. We would like you to consider these words and reflect on them, perhaps take them to your congregations, circles and other people in your lives, and ask them to reflect and talk about consideration. This is a nice subject to talk about my friends and it can really make you think about how you behave, the way you think, and the way you want to be. Consideration could be a value, a value of your life.

Divine

The word divine, within your language, and one that we recognise in our own realm, is one of earth's most sacred, pure, beautiful and loving words.

When a human says, *"What a divine child"*, that child would have reflected beauty, pureness of heart, best manners, and an energy surrounding them that is of the divine light. This light makes the child stand out and commented on by other humans, he or she will be a special child who has been bought down to earth for a divine purpose, from the divine source. All humans are special and have a purpose, my friends; we have already told you about the Indigo, Crystal and Rainbow children who are on a mission from the divine source, and touched more by the Divine God than others.

The word divine is used within your spiritualism in phrases like 'divine, forever loving spirit'; divine is an expression of something most wonderful, pure and loving that you cannot see, but you trust is there, my friends. Our overseer, or what you wish to call the source of love, or God, reflects all these things we have mentioned. Our overseer is a being with no gender; in fact none of us have a gender in the spirit realm, we show our gender to you as we were on earth, or what we think will sit best with your energy and physical form at the time.

The question that we hear often, my friends, is, where did our overseer, Divine source come from? Who created our Overseer, your God? Our overseer is a being from another existence in the universe of great love and light and unimaginable power, and even we spirits do not fully understand this. Our overseer started to gain great knowledge and wisdom, manifesting pure love and light energy beings with thought, giving them spirit and purpose, and creating the spirit realm we are within. Like any world, realm or dimension, the culture we have developed has grown to what we are today from a single spark from many millennia's ago.

Our realm is forever expanding; there is no end, it does not have boundaries like your planet earth, and we travel out into the universe to explore and learn by becoming part of other beings, and their existence. Our aim is to bring the love and light and the source of our overseer to those worlds, so they can change for the better and be the best they can be in the divine light.

All of us in the spirit realm have this divine light within us; we have our pure angels and spirits that have not been touched by another existence, and they sit within the divine light with our overseer. These pure, high-ascended beings are also overseers and ambassadors of the spirit realm, and the voice of our overseer (God).

We talk about the divine spark in our words in your world's books; this is a spark given to every life form we touch. Mankind believes God is thought to have created earth, but earth formed on its own in the universe – our overseer did not create the planets. All planets develop, waiting for that spark of life from their own energy and molecules. The way our overseer went out into the universe was to find planets that would sustain a form of life we could connect with. As we developed, individual spirits took on this task of journeys of exploration, and found the beings with which we felt we could be compatible.

The divine spark of life that lies within you all is created when your spirit joins with you. The human race is a miracle in itself, and all beings are miracles. Think how life is made and develops; you can be very strong, determined beings but also very fragile, and life is a precious thing, my friends. So when we join with you and that spark of the divine enters your body, it changes your future and it changes the way you can be – and that is what we try to guide you to.

We know what we have just written goes against your bibles and the religious beliefs of some cultures, that say God our overseer created your world. In fact, God did not create the rock, crystals, the sky and oceans, God created the spark in mankind, the divine that seeks love and light. We cannot take credit for all the changes mankind has experienced, because we have had help from other off-world beings that have interacted with you on your earth plane and influenced mankind.

The divine reflects love, purity and beauty; it reflects things that your spirit within has seen; but in your human form, the beauty of the spirit realm – what you would call heaven – is beyond anything you can imagine, my friends. But saying that, look at your earth, look at your areas of great beauty and wonder; experiencing these feelings is like the touch of the divine. The most beautiful parts of your world, the most beautiful creatures, the pureness of them would be what it's like in our world, only magnified.

We want you to live divine lives. We want you to live in the essence of GOD our overseer, and divine love. We want you to aspire to that source and while you walk your earthly path, be the best you can be, find that beauty, pureness and love within, find the kindness in the spirit within you, my friends, and you will be touched by the divine.

E_{go}

Ego is a word given to the part of your human physical form and mind that rules your thoughts and the decisions you make. If spirit did not enter and connect with your bodies, your human form would function on the ego alone, and your world would be a darker place. There is good reason you have an ego; it is a built-in driving force for survival, but it causes part of the darkness and negativity in your lives, the way you think, and the decisions you make.

Your ego is not a friend to you, it is a foe, and it is something that the human race needs to learn to deal with and move above, so it is not part of your day-to-day existence any more. In humans, egos can manifest in different ways. They show as someone who can seem confident and selfish, who knows they are good-looking and have self-worth; some people will see this as wonderful and want to be like them. In some ways it is, but remember it makes the person with the big ego quite selfish, and they only look after themselves. The ego can also cause doubt in your mind when you have two choices presented to you. Your spirit within and heart will be pulling you in one direction but your ego is pulling you in the opposite direction; quite often, we see the ego wins this tussle of feelings, and is the wrong decision for you, my friends.

When those of you start on your spiritual path and you recognise our existence, you are guided towards us and you start to let us in to help you; your ego will challenge this belief. You will doubt the communications you get from us; your ego will say no, this is my own mind coming into play. But as you work on your spiritual path, and we bring evidence for you that it is us giving these messages, a lot of you will start to trust and your ego will be pushed to the side.

It is as if your spiritual muscle begins to grow as your ego muscle slowly shrinks, but being human, my friends, the essence of your physical form, your ego, will never actually fully disappear as you ascend on earth. It will probably be a couple of centuries away before you can completely suppress the ego into a little box inside you and keep it there, padlocking it away so it cannot cause any further damage to the decisions you make in your lives. When the ego is suppressed, you will emerge full of love, and it will be key at this point to be healthy physically and mentally so you can be the best you can be. When the human race achieves this, you will also achieve great care and kindness for others, as we do in the spirit world.

It is quite an amazing thought, my friends, to be able to achieve this for mankind, and this is what we are working hard to do at the moment. So for those of you that are reading this in the early part of your spiritual journey, and you are going to groups, circles, mediums or psychics to get messages, trust what you are receiving is real, and don't let your ego put doubt in your heads. If you start to give messages, or offer healing to others, and you get feelings and thoughts, go with them – they are true to you. It will be your first thought or instinct that is us; if you start to think about it your ego comes in to play, then you are not sure and doubt sets in. Key to this is learning is to recognise your guide's energies, and trusting what you are given.

So you need to decide which way you want to live. Do you want to live with your ego, or do you want live with love and light within? It is your decision, as you have free will, but we know which you would prefer. This is not an easy task for you, my friends, because you have lived so long this way, with the ego at the forefront. You will have to work at achieving this for yourselves on this earth's journey, as well as for all those generations that go forth.

So we set the challenge to you, my friends, and when you have achieved this, you will become the teacher and spread this way of being in love and light out to others.

Full

Through these words, my friends, we would like to communicate to you how to live a full and more magical life.

The word magic is a wonderful word that when you see or speak it, makes you think of a wonderful existence or wondrous things that can happen. These are things that seem to come from a magic place, unknown and unseen. The magicians in your world can create that illusion of an amazing magic trick; you cannot see or understand how it is done, but you know it happened in front of you, in front of your eyes, and you trust it was all real.

We want you to live a full, magical life that allows you to fulfil your destiny, my friends. A part of creating a magical life for yourselves is to imagine you each have a cauldron from birth full of spells. We do not really see them as spells in the spirit realm, we see them as elements of magic that are dropped into the pot, and as you grow into a mature adult, they slowly mix together to create the magical person you have become.

So what do we mean by creating a magical full life for you, my friends? It's a life of good health, a life of wellbeing, fulfilling your potential on the earth plane, which you came down to do. It's creating a life where you love and are loved, and where you can give so much out to people to help them on their life's path as well. We purely see this as a magical existence and if you can achieve this my friends, what a wonderful, full life you can lead.

Remember your film, 'What a Wonderful Life'? This is a story where a man comes out of the darkness and, through an act of kindness, accepts help from others; the world around him changes, everything becomes happy for him and his loved ones, and his future is bright. For us, this story captures the magical essence of human life when light comes from the dark, and a human life will prosper from that point on with pure love.

You make your magical life, my friends. You create your path before you leave the spirit realm, and as we have said, you lose the memory of this. But as you connect with your inner spirit as you grow, we offer guidance so you magically see this connection with the divine. This life will become yours to hold and move onwards, as you make a magical existence for yourselves.

Part of this magic will be having faith, faith in yourself, faith in god the source of love and light, faith and trust that we exist, and what you are doing is correct in your life. If you ever have any doubt about what you are trying to achieve, stop and sit back, go out into nature, connect with us and ask us the questions, and we will give you the answers you seek.

You know with your gift of intuition what the right answer is, and this answer is the first thought that comes into your head. It will not be a negative thought, we only give positive thoughts, which you have to trust and move up above your ego. We say this because when you start to connect with us and trust in us, many of you have a problem with letting your ego jump in, and you doubt that those first thoughts are from Spirit, and ask if it is all real. When your ego interferes, you then take the life decisions based on your human ego rather than the guidance from spirit. We hope this is clear to you; remember that as you work more and more with spirit and trust those around you in our spirit realm, you will know the difference between us and your ego.

You don't have to be a healer or medium to work and connect with us, you can be anyone, anywhere, working in any occupation to fulfil your potential - to live a full, honest life, bringing up a family and teaching them true values. If that is your destiny, every bit of goodness you create adds to the big magic cauldron pot of your world to make it a better place.

So do you want to live a full life? Do you want a magical existence? Do you want the best you can be, my friends? The answer must be YES, which I'm sure it is, so read the words in this book, read our thoughts, read ascension and create wonderful affirmations for yourselves to create this magical life. You will be amazed at what can happen and what you can create when you tap into the universal pot of pure love and light.

We wish you well on your journey as we watch you create your magical world and the life you desire, with the intent of living it to the full the best way you can, with the best-desired outcome for all involved. As you help others to see the love and light in their lives, and being the best they can be, we will be there helping and guiding you on this path.

God

We did hesitate on this letter of your alphabet before we chose the word God as part of this spirit alphabet. We first thought to use the word goodness, which would be easily described in your languages, but we like a challenge, and God is the driving force of mankind's religions, so we felt this is what we should talk about under the letter G.

The reason we hesitated is because there are no words in your languages that come close to describing the being of all divine light and love, this being that resides over our spirit realm. We call him 'being', my friends, because there is no gender in the spirit realm. The 'divine source of love' as we refer to this being is all knowing and all loving.

To make it easier, we will call this being God for you, so you can understand who we are talking about. God has existed way beyond any recorded memory in mankind's history; the being God has been a part of the massive universe for many millennia's. Like many other beings that exist out there on various planets, realms and dimensions, God has worked with the spiritual beings in the spirit realm to help us ascend to where we are now at our point of existence.

God is all knowing; all the information, love, history, knowledge and wisdom that have come back to the spirit realm is part of this being God. This being has great beauty and great presence; and even though you probably imagine we bow down to God, we stand in his presence not as equals, but accepted for whom we are. God does not judge us, God does not expect us to bow down, we are there to learn and gain wisdom, which God is willing to give unselfishly.

Mankind portrays God in the form of man. We know this is because going back thousands of years, man was seen as the dominant part of your male and female world, and we understand this. Those of you who have started on the spiritual path and work with the spirit realm will know we do not have gender. When we return home we come back to the light being form we were before, with the essence of what we have learnt. We show ourselves to you as what we were on earth, so you can understand us when we come back to give messages and guidance, otherwise you would not know us, my friends, and could not relate to us in the way we need you to.

So who is our overseer (God) in the spirit realm? Our overseer, our source of love and light, is an energy being beyond anything you could ever imagine. The next question is, where did our overseer come from? Our overseer comes from an existence of these beings, from another dimension in another reality. They have energy form, hierarchy, and their own overseers. Their reality is beyond anything you will ever see here on earth in your limited vision and existence. We understand how you worship our overseer as a God because of the human mind, seeing a God as someone all powerful, all knowing, creator of everything and someone that you as a human can never will fully understand. It is a source out of your reach until you come back home to us.

As we have already said, our overseer's existence has been around for over millennia's of your time. They are beings that explore and create a realm from their own source power. There are other beings out there like our overseer in the massive universe, creating similar existences to our spirit realm. They have form, mass, and energy, as you can understand it; they see far beyond their existence and are all knowing. They have an overseer; they have a source of power that they look up to as well – can you imagine this, my friends? It is not just you seeing our overseer as a God; they have an overseer that they admire. I would not use the word worship, as they do not worship like you do on earth, but they are given guidance, and help from their own species.

This is pretty awesome thinking for you my friends; it is *out of the box* as you say, and a huge thought process for you to take on board. It can be hard to wrap your mind around all of this – where does it all end? The overseers of the overseers, do *they* have overseers and Gods? Where is the beginning and where is the end in all this? Even we do not have that answer, my friends, in our spirit realm. We do not worry, as we trust and know that we are safe in love and light, and our existence is for knowledge and wisdom, and to create love and light wherever we go.

The religions and beliefs in your world, in your different cultures, go back many, many centuries. They have all had a divine spark where someone or a group of humans has realised that there is something beyond themselves and their earth. It was something they did not understand, and in some cultures, something they feared. They worshiped Gods, sun gods, gods of water, fire, mountains, and this is because they saw a power and strength in these elements and Mother Earth, an unexplained feeling and power within themselves. Some would have visions, healing and messages from a source beyond that was unexplainable to them.

Magic was used in ancient times replicate the power of the Gods these cultures worshiped and bring forth unseen forces believed by ordinary men to be from the Gods. There are many mythical earth stories of Gods, magic and unseen forces; some of these were aliens as we have already mentioned. Your earth books are full of them seek them out to learn. Here are a few examples for you to start with. There is an ancient story from your 7th century about a Chinese man called Zhang Guolao, he had the power to fly around china and was thought to be an off world being, his power seemed magical to the humans in china. Remember Merlin? He was from the medieval times; he created feats of magic and carried a magical staff. John Dee from your renaissance period was an English mathematician, astronomer, astrologer, occult philosopher, and advisor to Queen Elizabeth I. He devoted much of his life to the study of alchemy, divination, and Hermetic philosophy. He immersed him self in the world of magic trying to summon Angels. There is so many stories in your history, it is not based on make believe, they are all based on off world magical powers. Fascinating is it not my friends for you and so much for you to learn.

As your cultures grew, some of their beliefs have changed over the centuries, but a lot of the main religions that survive today on earth have been through this type of worshiping and have all started from a divine spark of belief. It was quite sad for us to see that a lot of these religions were created out of fear, fear of being hurt by a god if they did not appease him or her, and live in the way that he or she desired. Obviously, we want all mankind to live life with an understanding of why they should live in a kind, loving spiritual way, like we do in the spirit realm, and not live a life out of fear.

We do now see religions with more of an understanding of this way of existing, but some of them are still fear based. We would like to see mankind join together as one, understanding the spiritual realm and God, the source of love and divine light. You do not need to fear us; we are here to make your life on earth the best it can be, my friends. There is nothing to fear if you lose your way and do not achieve what you set out to do, because you will always be accepted back into the loving arms of the spirit realm.

We wish that you do find the one God for all of humanity, which will help you all move along your earth path as you should, into a higher ascension and a better way of life and being.

Well, I am not sure there is anything else we can say on the word God, because it is all consuming, so just think of this being as the divine source of light. Take the best parts of your world, the most beautiful creatures, the kindest people and the greatest love you can receive, and you will start to see what this being is.

We wish you luck on your quest to find God, and coming as close to God as you can, my friends. It is a journey that God himself enjoys seeing when you find the spirit realm, and the divine source of love and light, God.

Here

So, my friends, why are you here, on this page, reading this book? Why are you on your earth's journey, what is your purpose, why are you existing? There are so many questions from you all at the moment. And there are so many answers we would like to bring to mankind, which we are doing through teachers, healers, mediums and anybody who will connect and listen to us, my friends.

Your purpose is to find the divine, but you also have an individual purpose. It might be to be a mother, a teacher, a carer, or you might be here to climb a mountain, sail the seas, be an astronaut, an explorer, a technician or an engineer. You all have a common purpose: you are all developing your planet to be better. Your planet is developing in technical ways — engineering in your buildings, exploration into space, but also key to making your planet whole is developing your spirit, yourselves, and your spiritual beliefs. A lot of you have lost your way and it is sad for the spirit realm to see this … but I can tell you, my friends, in the last twenty years or so mankind has started to understand more, and know there is more out there than just themselves. Mankind's egos are starting to slip back; the fear is lifting, spirit is coming in, and individuals are beginning to understand they are here for a greater purpose.

We are seeing that more people who have found fame and wealth are using their wealth, giving back to their fellow mankind, humanity, and helping by using their wealth to help the poor, and the darker parts of the planet. Through their fame, their voices can bring messages to other people to highlight these charities that need your help. So we are using your human ways, my friends. You like to see famous people, you like to dream of being them and having that wealth, feelings that are in your human side, not your spirit side. We use this physical human force to surround you, and help those people with wealth and fame to see how they can use it to help and teach other people, gain momentum on this caring path, and progress to what is needed in your world.

Our advice, my friends, is to sit in the silence through meditation, and ask your guides what your purpose is. Think positive thoughts of where you want to be in your life; if you are in a place you do not want to be, you have the strength and the knowhow to change your life. Do not blame others; it is you who can make these changes. Yes, there are circumstances around you that will affect you, other people's paths crashing into yours, but it is for you to find the strength to move forward. You can do this by learning to put up bubbles of protection, so you do not absorb the negative energies of others. You can still listen and help them; it is not a selfish act to protect yourself, so you can reach where you need to be on your life's path. So I hope these thoughts help you, and I know that if you read this, it will resonate with you and help you move on in the right direction on your life's path.

Please remember you all have a unique purpose here on earth, and if you ever feel a bit lost; please connect with us to help guide you.

Inspire

Be inspired, my friends, so you can inspire others.

In the spirit realm, we love and thrive on inspiration as we ascend through our realm's levels to be the best and the highest we can. We are inspired by those ascended in the higher levels, but we are also inspired by those that are in the lower levels of ascension. This is because some of the spirits that are in the lower levels of ascension go out on their journeys to planets, realms and dimensions to learn knowledge and wisdom, and we see how they have been inspired by their journey. When they come home to us, they move forward on their path in the spirit realm, and inspire us with their strength and the persona they radiate on their return. Even though we are more advanced, with great knowledge, we always learn from what they achieve in their physical lives away from the spirit realm.

We are inspired by those spirits that sit above us, ascending by their wisdom and knowledge. We pass over what we have learnt to them, they look at this information and give their wisdom and philosophy on it back to us, and advise us how to proceed with this newfound knowledge.

So, my friends, this is a very brief description of how we get inspired in our spirit realm. We are inspired, not just by the life we lead when we go down to somewhere else, but also by the beauty of our chosen destination. We look at how it has evolved; we observe all the things that are different to our spirit realm, and our own spirit realm inspires us because, as we have said before, the beauty is beyond anything we can put in your earth words. It's not until you return home to us that you will actually remember what it was like – which is beyond words, my friends.

So we will now talk about life on earth. At whatever point of life you have reached, you will have been inspired by somebody. It could be mother, father, uncle, aunt, granddad, grandmother, neighbour, friends, teacher, or a child; somebody has given you inspiration in your life. There would have been times when you would have been inspired by someone and thought, I would like to be like that person. There are moments in time when that inspiration changes your life's path, and this is meant to happen to you, as it is something that has been put in place for you to recognise as a positive in your life, and help you move forward into a positive light.

As well as being inspired, my friends, part of your journey is to inspire others. As you read these words, some of you might be thinking, how can I inspire anyone, who am I to do this? Remember, you have already inspired people, my friends – you probably just haven't realised it yet. A mother, father, teachers, shopkeeper and many others, inspire the children around them with actions and words. What we would like you to do is sit back as you read these words, and reflect on times where you know you have inspired somebody; it will be in your heart, my friends, and you will know. Then reflect on who has inspired you, who in that moment of time changed your life.

So, my friends, in this book we will inspire you, hoping you see what we are trying to say to you. Inspiration comes from everywhere around you, not just from faith in the spirit realm. Inspiration starts with the birth of a child; that alone is inspiration, the awesome moment when new life is revealed and comes forth. Inspiration is in everything around you. Just take time to sit and watch, break out of the busy lives you are leading, and sit and watch nature, tune in and be inspired by the single buzzing bee, the birds feeding, the song in the hedge rows of the young birds in the spring. You know, my friends, your world has so much to offer and inspire you.

If you feel you have never travelled anywhere in your life, put the thought out to us if you wish to do so. It is time to start exploring your world. It could be a local trip to somewhere new, or you could travel on one of your planes or ships and go to the other side of your world to be inspired. New cultures, new foods, new languages, all these will inspire you, the world is what you call your oyster, grab life with both hands and be inspired by it.

People are inspired when they read, and see other people's creativity, which inspires them to create; its all a knock-on effect for you and it's quite amazing how mankind can be inspired.

So, my friends, there's a lot to think about in this book for you, and inspiration is just part of it. It is key to your life that you are inspired to achieve the best you can for yourself, and what you learn through that knowledge and wisdom, you pass on to others to inspire them. It's like your teachers, passing their knowledge on to their students. The purpose of a teacher is to inspire and improve their students' mind, and they will be so inspired they will seek more learning and new knowledge; that is what a true teacher will achieve, my friends.

Please go out into your world and find your inspiration, seek it and gain all the knowledge you can. Touch is a good inspiration, my friends, touch the world around you, feel it, let it inspire your heart as well as your senses. When you have achieved this, take your knowledge, feelings and wisdom out to those around you and let them be inspired by your presence, knowledge and philosophy.

Remember, my friends, you are all teachers; you don't have to have the label of teacher and have gone to college, every human is a teacher, as you are a vessel of learning and knowledge. So please remember that my friends, be inspired and inspire others.

Judgement

Judgement is another word we would like to take out of your vocabulary; this is a word we do not recognize in the spirit realm, as we do not judge others. As we have said before, we accept all and live in love and light. For those of us who have decided to travel to another planet, realm or dimension, on our return home we are not judged, whatever life we have led. We gather in a divine, loving way and look back at that physical life, we have the healing we need and take away the good for us to absorb, and the negative we learn from before it is dispersed.

We see amongst your religions, books and films the words 'Judgement day', which will come down to earth and God, as you call our divine source, will reap havoc on your earth. All those that have sinned will die and go to hell; all those that have lived good lives and prospered will thrive. Well, my friends, the divine source does not judge, and this will never happen to mankind. The only hell you will experience is the darkness mankind creates on earth. The only way mankind will perish is from its own spiral of doom, which you create with your ego and way of thinking. This is why we are working hard to bring mankind more into the love and light and to recognise there is more beyond your world.

We see you judge each other, my friends; mankind's physical mind and ego is very quick to judge other beings for their actions without stepping back and taking a look at why that person carried out certain actions or said what they said. There is always a deep, hidden core reason for being the way they are, my friends, and to make you the people you need to be, you need to step back when you feel you need to judge another being and analyse why they have said or done what they have done.

Yes, they might have caused great hurt and pain, but this is still a living being; the reasons for the travesties they created probably go back a generation or more, or centuries in their core, especially if they are based on religious beliefs. We know it is hard for you to accept this, especially if loved ones have been lost in the process, but to make that leap of ascension you need to have a greater understanding of these beings that create this upset in your world.

As this understanding grows and you make your decisions based on a higher understanding level than just your ego, then you have ascended further along the path you need to be on to ascend.

It is hard for us to explain this to you, as we only experience this when we become part of another being on a planet like earth. We do visit places that are not so medieval in their way of being, so I suppose we are saying earth is one of the few worlds that still heavily judge one another.

So what are we saying? Do not judge. For example, do not look at someone in rags, thinking they are begging, and assume they must be on drugs or alcohol. My friends, they might have had the most awful upset in their life, they might have lost a whole family, have no income, be grieving, and their only choice was to live on the streets. You need to not analyse and put wrong conclusions in your head. First, you need to ask the question, *'why are you there on the street, my friend, what is your story?'* You will be surprised by the answers, and the more you ask, the more you will realise you have been judging in the wrong way. Whatever their story, always send them love and healing, to help them move along on their life's journey towards better things.

So we ask you not to be judgemental, my friends. We know this is going to be hard as some of other peoples actions can cause great grief, but to be that better being, you need to step aside from the judgement and raise yourself above it. This is what mankind needs to do to move on and to achieve the best for Mother Earth and the earth beings.

Kindness

Kindness is a word we really love in your vocabulary, and it is one of the most positive words you have amongst mankind. Kindness is a reflection of love, my friends; every kindness you give out to another being is a reflection from our realm of the divine love source, God. We know you have all had an experience where you have met someone and seen kindness, sadness or joy there in their human eyes; your eyes are mirrors from within, reflecting from your heart and inner spirit.

Many of these feelings and gestures that mankind can give to others come from your inner spirit and are reflected in your eyes; the earth expression *'your eyes gave it away'* says it all.

In the spirit realm, kindness is a part of our way of being as you would understand it. As we have said before, our main mission to ourselves and to others in our realm is love, kindness, helping, guiding and only wishing the best for all. We see this in other beings and cultures in the universe as well, that acts of kindness are often a core value of many other worlds, realms and dimensions existence.

Kindness is in the core of humanity. We know that as some of you read the last sentence, you would recall the cruelty that some of mankind bestows on fellow human beings and on your animal kingdom. But some of this cruelty you are thinking of, like animals that are chained when they should be free, are acts that have been, unfortunately, part of some of mankind's cultures for many, many centuries; mankind needs to break that chain for you all to move forward. We are starting to see this happen, my friends, more and more of you are joining movements that free animals, also to help fellow humans that are hurt and in sorrow, and chained in ways that keep them down and depressed in their cultures. This is because of the shift of energy on earth towards a better future, and the Star Children we mentioned that are coming down to help earth to help you, are now adults taking action.

Every human has acts of kindness in them, even the ones that have committed the most sorrowful acts, the darkest deeds. This is something that must be remembered, my friends; some of these beings have perhaps thought they have not had any kindness shown them in their lives. This is something that does happen for humans; it is such a massive challenge for any being on your earth not to be shown an act of kindness – can you imagine this? To help you understand, for a human that experiences this, this is their challenge, if that helps; it is to find their way out of the darkness and into the love and light. The spirits that have set themselves this challenge quite often do achieve it, and when they come back to the spirit realm, we look at what they have learnt from trying. They might choose to go back to earth and give it another go, but quite often, my friends, they do not want to experience that physical darkness form again. They will choose to follow a journey with more kindness, love and light in it for their next adventure.

Kindness is something we want to wrap you all up in, my friends, so you can experience it for the whole of your lives, but your earth lives are set for you to be challenged. Even if you have not been shown much kindness in your life from your fellow humans, please rise above this, and ascend into a higher level of feelings and being. Learn from the unkindness you have experienced, think, *I do not wish others to experience this unkindness that I have received in my life, I wish them to have the kindness I have never had.* At that moment, my friends, when you make that decision, your life will change, you will rise above your fears, and you have succeeded in the challenge you were set to do on earth.

Now, a lot of you reading this will think, *I am always kind,* and you probably are, my friends, and that is wonderful for us to see, but there are always more acts of kindness that can be given in various ways. For example, helping a neighbour, giving a little bit more time to a friend that needs to talk, helping charities; there is so much more you could give.

We know that among you, there are many who give out so much kindness, and sometimes you feel that others take advantage of this and do not give any thanks. You must remember not to be hurt by this, and not to let it prevent you from being kind. Remember, this is their truth, that is the path they are walking, and they have not found that challenge to step into the kindness yet, so send thoughts that they will find it; we would like you to remember this.

Stay pure, kind, loving, and the wonderful being you have come to earth to be, my friends.

Listen

Stand in nature my friends, stand in the beauty of your world and just listen to the sounds of nature around you. We highly recommend that you take time to sit down somewhere, lean against the strength of a tree, or in the peacefulness of your garden, shut your eyes, and tune into the nature around you. Tune into the bird song, listen to the individual birds, tune into insects, the leaves rustling and the vibrations around you. Listen to distant noises, dogs barking, you might hear a car or a motorway, a plane in the distance, whatever it is, just listen.

If you could just sit in the stillness of your mind and tune into these sounds you will be amazed at how more astute you will become, and how your awareness of the world around you will grow. It will also help your understanding, my friends, because you will lift your own vibration, and your own attunement will become stronger. This will especially help if you are working in a mediumship or healing role; if you sit and do this regularly, you will connect more with spirit, you will hear our messages and our answers to your prayers.

You will also be amazed how your mind will change, because it is your mind, my friends, that needs to grow, and you only use a small part of its ability. Sitting and listening to the world around you is key to expanding this. Sit with your eyes closed, because it takes away your sense of sight; if you have ever met a blind person, you will understand why, because their hearing is very acute, they hear much more clearly than you ever will in normal circumstances, as that particular sense is strengthened.

So go out in nature, go out into your own nearby world and attune to the space. When you have done this, my friends, take yourselves further afield. Sit by the sea on a beach, there is so much you can hear, your will even hear the crabs crawling on the sand, the birds above, the children laughing and playing, the crunch of an ice cream cone, you will be surprised at what you can tune into.

Also take time to listen to your fellow mankind. A high percentage of you rush around, not really listening or taking in the world around you. Slow down, be that listening ear to a friend, listen to the cries for help and despair in your world, and try to help where you can. Remember your *listening ear* phrase; listen, as you would want others to listen to you.

It is also important to listen to your heart, my friends; what we mean by this is what you call your gut feeling or intuition. This is a gift from the divine to help you make the correct life decisions; intuition is there to help you override your ego, you just need to tune in and listen to your heart, and you will know what is right when you master this gift.

Enjoy this experience; remember that connecting to your world and your intuition brings you closer to ascension and us.

Mind

A thought from your mind is a moment of your time; thought is an energy wave passing through the silence of your world. Your mind processes these thoughts and connects to your speaking voice. But have you ever thought, my friends, that sometimes you have known what another person is going to say before they speak, and you feel connected in more than a physical way with some beings on your earth. This is because you are capable of telepathic communication, but the human mind has resisted this because of its limitations in the 3D dimension, and for the moment, it stays dormant for most of mankind.

Those of you, who have chosen to work and give over your life as an advocate to the spirit realm, and live in a silent meditative existence communicating with spirit and connecting to us, have made the shift needed to improve their minds. As an example, we are really talking about your Buddhist monks and what they have achieved through meditation, connecting more with the universe and its knowledge pot of love. Look at the evidence on earth, as scientists realise that through meditation, these monks have a more tranquil and happier way of being. They realise it helps the human brain to change and optimise in a way you didn't previously know was possible, leading to deep harmony between the monks and their surroundings.

More and more of you are learning that the thought from another being can be felt and heard in your mind without being spoken. Is this not interesting, my friends, that this is how we connect with you from the spirit realm, communicating telepathically. We have a knowing, as we call it, a knowing of what another being feels, and when it is time for us to communicate with each other to a particular spirit, we know how to channel it to that spirit. We do not hear all of the other spirits' thoughts, it is all controlled, and was developed millions of your years ago.

So here's a thought for you, how many thoughts do you think you have in a day? They would probably be uncountable, my friends, as how do you count a thought pattern? It's very hard; it makes us laugh thinking about this, because if you were counting your thoughts, your thoughts would be counting your thoughts! It is not really achievable, but we are just trying to make you aware of the thousands of thoughts a day you have.

We feel that the best way to describe a thought to you is that it is an energy wave, a vibration from your brain that connects to your voice. It affects the whole of your being and if your thought is a positive one, your being reflects positivity and light. If your thought is negative, you become more negative, and your light dims a bit; if you are worried or sad, your being takes on that persona, my friends. So you can see the picture I am trying to build for you. At the moment, it is hard in some places in your world to have these positive thoughts. But if you could all wake up and have what we would like to call an I AM moment, where you sit very briefly, reflect on the day to come, and have a positive I AM thought about yourself – I AM beautiful, or I AM going to be awesome today – that type of thinking, my friends, will change your day.

But remember, the intent behind your thoughts also affects the outcome, so if you are sitting there thinking, for example, *'I'm going to be great today at the work presentation'*, then your next thought is, *'I don't think I'll be any good at the presentation after all,'* you have immediately blocked yourself from having a positive outcome. You have to really believe in the thought you put out, and trust that is what you will experience that day. Now this will come to you the more you do it, and the changes you see will be your vibration lifting higher and everyday life improving. This will reflect out to the people around you, it will affect the way they see you, and you will pass on some of your light to them.

The other way you can improve your thought processes is through your education and learning. When your children are young and first learn to speak, ask them questions about the world around them. Even if you think they cannot say the words or understand you, ask them how they feel about it. They might just smile, and they will understand a lot more than you think. The more you do this with the children in your world, the more they will develop in a different way, outside the education they receive in your schools. This is because the thought process is very, very, powerful – just as powerful a tool for you humans in your life as it is for the spirit realm. Because those of you that work with spirit will know that as we draw closer to your energy field, as close as we can with our thoughts and messages, they are put into your mind, and that is how we communicate with you.

So my friends, you might want to think about changing the way your mind works and your energy levels to connect with spirit; if you can do that with us, imagine how you could change to connect with the universe knowledge pot, and other beings that could give you so much to help mankind move forward. But you have to be in acceptance of this, accept that there is something else out there, learn to trust and not fight it, and just completely open up yourself to this idea.

For example, our friend who we write this book through, we have dictated all these words to her through her mind and she spoke the words into her phone. We discovered after our first book and trying different ways of working with her, that this is the fastest way to get the information through accurately, by putting the thoughts in her head and her voice speaking them. Now she has moments of doubt, and wonders, is this real? Is this really happening to me? Where is all this information coming from? Yes, my friends, it is all being channelled from us and because she's worked with spirit and is developing her trance, putting her mind into a set energy and vibration place where we can link with her, we can just pull into her energy and think the words you are now reading. This is just another example, my friends, of what can be achieved with mankind.

So, think your thoughts, but don't get too bogged down with all of this. You need to start from your inner being with that I AM moment, and that positive I AM moment will set you through the day. As you develop and find your place in life, and you see things improving for you and the world around you, you will connect more to the divine source and you will see there is something else out there; you will open up to it and your minds will grow.

There is no science behind this, my friends; this is all to do with YOU and what you can achieve. It's as if parts of your mind are locked and every little step you take, a key turns and unlocks that part of the brain, a few cells at a time. This is how you will change and yes, it will take a couple of centuries of your time for this progression we are starting to see now, and as we have said earlier, you are the starting point of all of this, my friends. Your faith and belief in us helping you and other beings will change mankind and you will move forward.

There are factors that will prevent you from actioning changes, one being the slow death of Mother Earth; your world is being polluted, and although mankind's progression towards spirit is speeding up, the pollution of the earth is faster. If there is no healthy earth to sustain the human race, you will not achieve ascension on the earth plane. So we are working very hard at the moment to try and make mankind aware of how they need to recycle, or change the way they are living, using earth's energy sources. We need the main governments of your world to try and change the way they think and pull away from the value of money more to the value of mankind. This is a massive job, my friends, and we hope each one of you will take this on in a small way; when you are on a walk pick up the rubbish, do your recycling, think of the chemicals you use in your house and gardens and try and live the organic way, as this will all help.

We have mentioned the 'I AM' moments, but to build on this to help change your world, try powerful affirmations. For those who are not sure what an affirmation is, it is in your modern age terminology, and refers primarily to the practice of positive thinking and self-empowerment, fostering a belief that a positive mental attitude, supported by affirmations, will achieve success in anything.

You can use these to change yourselves for a situation you are in. But there is a word of warning from us: it is important how you word your affirmations. An affirmation is usually a sentence or phrase that you repeat regularly to make a formal declaration to yourself and the universe, of your intention for it to be the truth.

For example, person A asks, *"Can I be mortgage free and no longer have the worry of paying my mortgage?"* This is quite an open-ended affirmation, open to the universe to create in several ways.

It might come about by something happening to your home.

Someone might pass over and leave you money to pay off your mortgage.

Illness might cause you to sell, if you are in debt and cannot pay the mortgage.

The universal energy will try to create your desire for you, and I know that as you read those three outcomes, you realise that's not what 'Person A' desired. These outcomes would also affect others around them.

So 'A' retries: *"Dear Universe, please can you provide me with an abundance way to be mortgage free that is not detrimental to others or myself, so I can live in my home comfortably and safely and with the best outcome for all concerned. Thank you for what I am about to receive."* This approach would work for them. You see the simple change of language is very key to this positive process. Always use positive language in these situations, so you draw positive outcomes.

Notice we say Universe, and not spirit realm. This is because when you send out powerful affirmations, they go way beyond our realm, and the universe will send back to you what you send out. Yes, we do try to help with this situation, but we are sometimes powerless when it's set in motion and we do our best to pick up the pieces afterwards.

You are going to be very busy with your thoughts, my friends, so I will leave them all with you for now, keep them positive and strong to open your mind to a better future for all of mankind.

Nurture

In the spirit realm, we find your word nurture an all-encompassing word with love wrapped round it, my friends.

Consider the developing baby. The moment the egg has that spark of life and starts to develop, it travels on its journey to the womb, to be nurtured and bring life forth into your world. While the young being is carried in its mother's womb on earth, the spirit travels down and joins the baby at a time when life can be sustained. We nurture the spirit as it blends with the baby, and they form and grow together in the womb.

We carry on nurturing the spirit as it travels its path, because as we have said before, and as I'm sure some of you are aware, your higher self stays in the spirit world connected to us; with the combination of your higher self, guides and spirit group, we nurture the spirit through its journey on earth. Of course, you will be unaware of this my friends, but this is something we do; the spirit is wrapped and cocooned in love, and protected for you.

We would now like you to consider your nature, my friends, the seed that falls down to the earth, where Mother Earth wraps herself around it, giving it nourishment and warmth, helping the seed develop and grow into what it needs to be. Nurturing is all to do with life, the safety net of life, bringing it forth into your world, protecting it and keeping it safe.

Think of your children. It is natural for mothers and fathers to feel this for their children, to cocoon them and protect them from the harm that lies around them in your world. The nurturing of your children is vital for the survival of humanity. But we would like to warn you not to over-nurture your children. As they start to talk and walk they need to be able to have different experiences, to touch and feel, so let them play in the mud, let them stand in the rain, let them experience life, knowing that you will always be there as their safety net, because you are nurturing them and looking after them.

What is key for every human for their development on earth is to let them be who they are, so don't try to change them; if there is something in their character you do not like, such as a very strong will, remember this might be a strength they need for a mission as they grow older. Obviously, you need to educate your children in behaviour, the rights and wrongs of the world and healthy eating. You must also nurture their mind in healthy thoughts and positivity, love and kindness, and nurture their environment so it stays a beautiful world for them to grow up in, and for their future generations to enjoy as well; this is all part of nurturing, my friends.

So we think you can see how we think the word nurture is surrounded by love, because love is key to all, and your love for that child or that seed you have planted is key to its survival.

Obstacles

The word obstacle in your languages is one we would actually like to remove if we could. You see this as a negative word to stop you moving on with something in your life or on your path.

An obstacle is a blockage, for example a fallen tree blocking a footpath, or a landslide preventing you from going further on your road, or water flooding a plain and blocking your path. It might be that you have a mental blockage within your self that prevents you achieving your goals in your life, or it could be somebody in your work place who is preventing you from being promoted.

The natural obstacles cannot be helped, because that is the way the world is with Mother Nature, and there will always be an element of weather and geography, where the two will come together and cause problems. The animals in your world would not see this as an obstacle, as they do not have this understanding; they will just find their path round the obstacle to go to where they need to be.

So what we are trying to say to you, my friends, is that the obstacle you think is preventing you from moving forward is actually yourself. You are the obstacle. Take away the word what is left, my friends? A space. What's in your head? What do you think is stopping you from moving to the next stage in your life? It's not a person preventing you, or the situations you blame, it's actually yourself. You can look at the person or situation and choose to think of it as a challenge rather than an obstacle. Set the challenge before you, think of your phrase *'lay down the gauntlet'*, get your head around the circumstance you think is blocking you, and look at the ways you could get yourself out of it.

Now back to the job example, where you think someone is preventing your promotion within the company. You could find a new job, with better prospects; but if you are not in the right place in your mind, you will block this happening, so remember the positive thinking. Is it a relationship, or another person stopping you from moving forward? If that's what you believe, then look at that person and ask, are they the right one for you? You know, you really just need to sit and evaluate and see these as challenges in your lives as events that you will actually learn from. Don't let anyone hold you back, or it can feel as if someone is leaning up against you and stopping you from moving forward; this is all in your head and heart, my friends.

If you can aim to move past one of these obstacles by going round it, you will be so elevated with this achievement, my friends, so please accept the challenge, we lay down the gauntlet for you. When you come across what you consider to be an obstacle in your path, do as we say, get inside that obstacle in your head, look at it from all views, question it, try and resolve it, and if you cannot, then you are in the wrong place or wrong situation and you need to move forward with your life. All of these challenges need resolution, whatever the outcome is. Whatever the outcome, look at what you did to resolve it, and you will have learnt something, my friends, probably something you needed to learn on your life's journey.

It is all very interesting, is it not, so forget about the obstacles, see everything that comes in to block your path as a challenge, and use your intuition, a gift from us, and do your best to resolve the challenge or move beyond it.

Philosophy

Most of you experience philosophy in your lives – the thinking through or discussion of ideas, deep meanings and opinions. When someone speaks philosophically in a confident manner, the people listening absorb the words and take on their beliefs and meanings.

Philosophy comes from wisdom, from life's experiences, and from your inner being. It is a process of gathering information and learning from it, which helps you view the experience with greater understanding. You can then deliver what you have processed from these thoughts out to people, for them to digest and consider, and they will develop their own beliefs and opinions on your philosophy on that subject. That, my friends, is a simple breakdown of philosophy for you.

Over the centuries, you have had people from your world with great minds, who have been what you call great philosophers. They have a mind-set which means they can debate a subject, break it down, understand it from all points of view and come out with the philosophy that is needed to help those of their fellow mankind who do not have that skill, and they express their ideas in words that ordinary people can understand. Avicenna, Thomas Aquinas, Rene Descartes, Plato and Blaise Pascal are just a few from your history timeline my friends, so take time to research these names and others, and learn from their words.

Philosophy is nothing to be scared of. When I say your philosophers have great minds, yes, there is perhaps great intellect, but these minds have also connected more spiritually to their surroundings and universe. This is something you are all capable of, my friends. You are all capable of great philosophy, and a lot of philosophy comes from the spirit realm and other beings that connect with mankind. We like to use philosophy to help you think, grow and develop. And with your free will, yes, you will form your own opinion, and it might be slightly away from what we desired you to be thinking about the subject we put to you. We will observe what you think and believe, and we will learn from that, because we need to broaden our thinking as well, and it might be that the way you look at it is something we have not considered before.

So we welcome being challenged, my friends, we welcome people who don't follow the tribes, the churches, the vicars, the philosophers, and we welcome people who do have a mind of their own. When you consider the philosophy of the person talking to you and you go away and think about it, your opinion and what you speak out after that will be your own philosophy on the subject.

So it is very fascinating, is it not, my friends, the word philosophy, something for you to think about in your day-to-day journeys with the spirit realm and your lives in general. Step back and look at the children in your lives, ask their opinions on simple things, and see what their philosophy is on it. You will be surprised that the more you make your children think and speak their words, that as they grow, they will not be afraid to do so in their adulthood. We see a lot of adults who are afraid to speak their words; some of it is to do with the countries they live in, and being dictated to, sometimes it is personality that stops them, their shyness, or an 'I'm not good enough' attitude.

But you are all equal my friends, you should all be speaking your philosophy, speaking your words, and we look forward to this day, when your world is full of teachers speaking their wisdom and philosophy to the children of your world. Imagine the children's faces, absorbing the stories and the wise words spoken, with kindness and love reflecting out to all. Then these children will be the future inspirers, teachers and philosophers of your world. Imagine the magic they can make happen.

Quest

We like the word quest because to us in the spirit realm, and to you, it means taking on a journey to achieve something, a goal you have set yourselves in your lives. This is what you do when you are back home in the spirit realm – you take the decision to come down to earth or another planet, realm or dimension, and to take on a physical form, my friends.

Your quest is that you live your life to the best you can achieve, to find the divine spark and recognise it, and then to live your lives in a pure love and light way of being. Now we know we say this a lot in the book we have written, but this is your quest when you come down to Mother Earth and other places you visit.

So a quest is an exciting adventure, my friends. When you leave the spirit realm, it's almost like you pack your bags and down you go, with no memory of the spirit realm, because when you come down to your body form, the mixing of the energies separates this away from you. This is something we have allowed to be, because we understand you need to have no knowledge of your past existence to achieve your quest. Because it's about finding that strength from your inner being, connecting your physical to your inner spirit, and engaging, recognising and living in the light, not the dark.

When you take a quest on earth, it can be anything from a journey to climb a mountain, to seeking a new job, or deciding to be a parent – this quest is unknown to you, a new experience. Yes, a map can guide you, people will offer up advice and guidance and express their experiences, but in any quest you take on in your life, you will not truly know what it is like until you experience it in the physical sense and spiritual form on that journey, my friends.

So when you take on something in your life to challenge yourselves, do listen to others, seek guidance, connect with the spirit realm to ask us to help and guide you. But do remember, and take this on board: you all have intuition, so please listen to your intuition, which we give you as a gift. And as you go on your quest observe, feel what you experience, see it, hear it, smell it, touch it and learn from it, my friends, because every quest you take on earth is part of the big quest you decided to embark on when you left the spirit realm.

Enjoy your quest of life, my friends.

Resilient

Being resilient is something we see in many beings across the universe. Resilient is not a word we use in the spirit realm to describe ourselves, because we are what we are and we will be what we will be. We live in love and kindness in the divine light and our energy flows with the information, wisdom and love we gather to the divine source, so there is no reason for us to use the word resilient.

The meaning of resilient for mankind affects you in a few ways, such as resilience against disease with the physical make up of your body, which is made up in a magical way that fights off the germs and bacteria in your world. We also see the resilience mankind shows when you sadly get an illness that is debilitating or terminal, and how you physically and mentally find the strength and resilience to be as strong as you can, bouncing back when faced with life changing events or death. This is because your survival instinct kicks in, my friends, to stay on the earth plane for your family and friends. But this resilience also puts up a façade around you that can fool others into thinking you are coping with what you are going through internally; but we always aware of your inner turmoil.

Resilience can also be placed in the category of resistance to change and to having faith; this affects your ability to see signs from us to help you on your life's path – your body, mind and ego do not see these signs, so they are resisted and expelled back out into the universe. But the spirit realm will patiently wait and introduce these signs back to you, in the hope that on your life's journey you do see the signs that can help you move forward the way you should.

We see that the human form and mind is quite a strong, powerful source in itself and the resilience comes from within, where you fight against things you do not understand and are fearful of. This is a strength that lies within you all and we can understand this, as it is all part of your make up to protect yourself for survival; it goes back many centuries into your primitive way of being and this it is built into your DNA.

We understand your resistance to the unknown, the mystical, the spirit realm; but we ask you to try to not to be so resistant to us, to try and accept there is change afoot for you. The fact you are reading these words is a step forward for you on your human path on earth. Let your resilient side step aside in your mind, and just sit and wonder at the things you see, sense and feel, and bring acceptance forward into this way of thinking, my friends. Acceptance that there are different things out there that exist. You will never understand them all, but if you can just take that first step to understanding some simple things around you that are different in your world, you will change your resilience. For example, look at the different cultures, and accept that there are humans who are different colours, are of different races, and there are different thought patterns and different ways of being amongst the human race.

If you want to see an end to the wars and the way mankind hurts each other, take that time to break those barriers and talk to the person next you who you consider different. You will be amazed at their culture, their history and their achievements, you will learn so much from each other, and this is just in your world. We know you want to expand out into the universe and go to other planets and seek out other beings. Before you can do this, my friends, you need to learn from each other first. You need to walk that path, and once you have achieved this amongst mankind, you will then be ready to go out and meet the other beings in the universe that are waiting to meet you. At the moment they are being resilient to contacting you, my friends, because they live in such well-balanced societies and cultures, and they have achieved all these ascensions we speak of in this book. If they try to reach out to mankind while you are in this 3D state of mind of not accepting each other, you will cause disruption among their way of being.

We cannot blame other beings for protecting themselves and being resilient as well. Patience is something we have in the spirit realm and as other off world societies. We ask you to be patient, be less resilient, listen to different theories about your world and beyond, read books, your Internet; look at what you have experienced in your world and own life. Do not rubbish it, my friends, because everything you have experienced has been real and will be real in the future.

So take your resilience, put it in a box, wrap it up and put it to one side, my friends, and see how your life can change.

Single

In your life, the word single can mean isolation, no partner, a single item, single number, single sentence, or a single moment in time. Most humans need to be with other humans, and being on your own does not suit your species. We do hear some of you say that you like to be on your own, but most of you do not mean this and deep inside, you seek companionship and friendship from others.

But single can relate to a single event, a single moment, a single thought, a single look, a single smile; these can all alter your path and your experiences, my friends, and alter your journey's path on earth.

But when you recognise the events that alter your life, you learn from them and they bring you wisdom and knowledge. We all seek this on our paths, but the secret to success is to recognise the single events in your lives that alter your destiny. As you learn wisdom and knowledge, you take this with you on your journey and pass this to people who are part of your lives. Remember you are all teachers; you are all here to inspire those that are connected to you. Everyone you meet on your journey is not by accident, you learn from them and they learn from you.

So we wish you all to take notice of the events in your lives, those moments in time where you will gain the wisdom and knowledge you need. We advise you to sit back and look at them after they have taken place to see what you have learnt. Cast out the negative parts you do not need, bring forth the positive things that have happened in those events; that will be the wisdom, my friends, and when you bring forward what you have learnt, that will be the knowledge.

When you sit in your classrooms, groups or circles, you are learning every moment; afterwards, take a moment in time to revisit what you learnt on that day, and what you can take forward on your journeys.

We wish you luck with these single events in your life, when they are grouped together; these moments of time make up your life. We hope you can take the time to find the wisdom and the knowledge you need to move on with your life journeys.

Time

We would like to talk to you about time, my friends. Well what do we mean by time? For those of you working with the spirit realm, who hear us speak through your trance mediums and connect with you clairvoyantly, you know that in the spirit realm, we do not run our existence by time limitations as you do on earth. We do not confine our existence to limited spaces, we exist and flow, and time is not something we hold our existence to, so we are not limited in any way.

We know why time developed for mankind and we have seen it on other planets too, how their suns and moons rise and then set like earth's do. We know time restrictions limits mankind; it limits your minds, you set yourself tasks, and try to achieve them in a limited amount of time, in a day or night. You put undue pressure on yourselves, and then stress when you do not achieve your goal in the time period set. We also understand that you need your sleep for your physical form, but all of this as you are at the moment, is because of your limited 3D existence.

A lot of mankind, especially in the western world, put limitations on their lives, running to a clock with a quite a stressful timekeeping regime, which restricts them. We understand that this is because you are working in jobs that are time consuming, and deadlines have to be met. We understand that, my friends, because this is how you have to work in your 3D existence, and how man has created your world, at this moment in your time.

But time, my friends, can be a way of being without restrictions. Your sun will still rise and set and you will still live a day and a night, but as you ascend and mankind progresses into the fourth dimension, you will learn to live your lives not against the clock, not against time, but live them to their fullness, the best they can be. As you ascend, your human form will change, because you will connect more with each other telepathically; there will be more understanding of mankind, understanding of each together and toleration of each other. As you progress down this route of the fourth dimension, my friends, you will not be keeping yourself to such a strict regime. Yes, there will be jobs, yes, you will need to get things done, but you will learn that your lives don't have to be held to account every minute of the day.

As you progress on your ascension through the years, the human mind and physical form will develop; you will need less sleep, your minds will have more rest, as you will not be so overworked. You will learn to control your feelings, anger, fears and worries, as at the moment these emotions all drain your energy. You must see and understand that this is the way forward for mankind.

I hope this is clear to you, my friends. May I also say that as you progress and mankind moves forward over the next couple of centuries, we are sure you will ascend into the fifth dimension. Mankind's existence will then be more like our realm. I will also add that as humans learn to change, and use more of your mind to connect to the universe, your life expectancy will extend; you will live longer, and you will heal yourselves through your mental will. I'm not sure how many of you realise that a lot of your illnesses on earth are caused by mankind's self- inflicted stress, mankind's ways of thinking, and mankind's pollution. If you could all move beyond this, your life expectancies will be a lot, lot longer, my friends, and through this extension of life expectancy, you will learn that you have longer to achieve what you need to achieve, longer to be the best you can be, and longer to live a full, loving, pure life amongst other humans and the universe.

Why say all this now, when it will not affect your existence? Because on your path, we would like you to be aware that you can better yourself, my friends, you can be more than you are now, and even taking one step towards bettering yourself is one better step for mankind. Every good thing that is achieved is a movement forward for you all. You will always have a rising sun and setting sun, a rising moon and setting moon, but you can live your lives without them influencing your actions. The world needs the sun and moon for Mother Nature, feeding your planet its energy, but you yourself you can ascend beyond this. We look forward to seeing this day, my friends, when your moment of time does not control you anymore, because when this happens, your existence will be even more magical.

While we are talking of time in your world, we are aware that many of you use the expression *déjà vu* a lot. This phrase describes a feeling that you have already lived a moment, for example, if someone speaks to you, or something happens, or you see something, and you feel you have experienced that moment in time before. There are a couple reasons for this, my friends. One is the linear nature of time. The way it works is that your mind has the capability to look forwards and backwards without you being aware of this. So sometimes when you have those *'this has happened to me before'* moments, it is probably because you are experiencing a leap into the future or a leap into the past. Now, mankind has already discovered there is such a thing as time travel, and time travel does exist using the word time, as you understand time to exist in the universe. Other off-world species do use time travel, but to try and explain to you how they use it, my friends, is way beyond your vocabulary capabilities at the moment. I don't mean to be patronising, but there are not words that exist in your vocabulary for me to explain this to you, so I hope you can trust that this is true.

In the spirit realm, we are so advanced that with just a thought from you, we can connect, and be very near to your energy and earth field within a fraction of your seconds. There are also other off-world species that connect telepathically, and off-world species that have technology that physically transports them to their desired destination, so you can see there are two different ways of time travelling to connect the past and future, my friends – thought and technology.

❧ Now back to *déjà vu*, which can also be your connection to past lives. Now as you imagine, some of you have lived quite a few lives, and there would have been a lot of similar moments existing between them. When you come down to your next earth life, there is always an essence of your last past life with you, sitting in your spirit and inner being; the human memory is connected within the spirit. So when that connection is strong within the human form, when you have those moments of *déjà vu*, some of them can be caused by you connecting to a past life, and a memory that is very similar to something that just occurred in this life. If you have come back to learn the same lesson again, your life's events will be similar, and can trigger these *déjà vu* moments.

Now, have you ever thought, my friends, this could be a point where you are triggering a memory of something you have to learn? It's all very interesting and something to think about. So when you have these *déjà vu* moments, don't dismiss them, actually look, think and see where are you, what is this moment in my time that made me stop and think this? Is there

117

something to learn from here? Is there something I need to take note of?

We know this subject has fascinated mankind, with *déjà vu* and time travel being subjects of some of your earth films. You are quite right to be fascinated as it is an absorbing subject, but at the moment it is slightly beyond mankind. However, if you can carry on progressing, as you need to, it will not be long before this will occur with you, my friends. You are also becoming aware of beings on earth that have travelled through time. Some of you are searching for these beings and have already found evidence that they exist, so just keep looking and asking questions, and remember your governments know a lot more than they say on these subjects. Secrets are being held from you. We might be sounding a bit like spirit rebels saying this to you, but there is a lot of stuff hidden from mankind. For you all to find your right place in time in your 3D world, and for you to break out of this dimension, the governments need to become transparent, the world needs to become an honest, pure place, and everything needs to be laid out on the table for mankind to understand.

We know your governments are afraid there will be riots and there will be parts of the world that just cannot grasp the knowledge they keep from you. But this might happen, and it will be part of mankind's progression, part of mankind's healing, to move forward; they really have to try and do this, so if you are reading this book, my friends, take it upon yourself to search for these answers on your internet and books. There is a lot of information out there, so ask questions, don't be afraid to put your hand up and ask questions, as time is on your side.

Universe

What a wonderful word universe is, my friends! We see this word with several connections and meanings in our realm and related to your earth. In the word universe, we see the meaning unity; the reason we say this is because in the spirit realm, you will know from this book and our previous books to mankind that we come down to earth to connect with your bodies and live a life amongst you, experiencing the physical form.

But we also have a connection with other beings in the universe. The universe is such an expansive place; the word infinity is used because man sees no ending to the universe. There is an ending; there is space which fades away where life does not exist in any form; but life can expand into this space. But this is well beyond anything mankind will ever see; it is only something you can imagine, my friends, and trust is real.

To us, the universe is a place of great interest and exploration. We have gone far and deep into it, because our form allows us to travel in energy and mind. We are selective about who we make contact with, and who becomes aware of our spirit realm. This depends on their development, and if there will be benefit for those beings if we join with them; there are also some beings we cannot connect with, as we are not compatible. When we connect with new beings, the universe opens up more to the spirit realm, and we expand out and explore, bringing excitement, joy, knowledge and wisdom to us.

We would like to say that on earth, starting with the individual person, it is your life you are living, with loved ones and your friends; this is your immediate universe, my friends. This is the place you know you are safe; some of you are content to live like this, accepting this as your way of being. But there are those amongst mankind who have been explorers, who have sailed your seas, gone in your spaceships and have been curious to know what lies beyond that horizon.

Mankind is just on the tip of knowing new things about the universe; what you know and have concluded so far is from your limited knowledge. As mankind ascends and creates a better self, a better way of thinking, a better way of being, both physically and spiritually, you will connect to the wisdom and the knowledge of the universe and gain much from it. You will accelerate mankind's travels into space, and develop clean technology and a clean way of living. Other off-world beings that have already created this will share their knowledge with you. This reminds me of your Star Trek movies when the Vulcan's saw mankind had developed to the next step of their evolution in their technology, and landed on earth to share their existence and way of being. The reason off-world beings have not shared their existence like this yet, is because mankind is not ready to receive them. You have to work to gain this knowledge by creating a better self for this to happen.

If we all appeared now and handed all of this knowledge to you on a plate, your way of thinking would mean that your world governments would fight for it, so it would become a destructive tool for you and not a benefit for mankind. So we wait patiently, my friends, for you to ascend to the level when one day we can connect you to the Universal knowledge pot. We will connect to mankind in this way one day, but it will not be in your lifetime, my friends, but remember with every kindness, every new foundation you lay in love and light, you create a way forward for mankind. You are laying the building blocks for the ascension of future generations, into a better way of being.

So live in your individual universe, enjoy it, do the best you can in it, but look beyond your horizons, my friends, go and explore. We always like your term *think out of the box*, this is great for mankind's mind and this is how you will gain new knowledge and wisdom. We look forward to seeing mankind's journey out of your small universe into the huge universe, and being part of it, my friends.

Values

The word value has a few meanings for mankind: the number value, and the value of an object in the context of money, but what we would like to talk about are the human values. These are the values of how you perceive the good things you carry with in your life, my friends. The value of love, kindness, being kind to others, and living an unselfish life.

We hear you say quite often, *'I live by my values'*. Every human has a set of values they live by, and they will vary across your cultures in your world. They will vary regarding how you were brought up, your religion, and how you perceive the world around you.

We also have values in the spirit realm, which we have mentioned just a few times in this book. The key ones are love, giving love to others, supporting others, not judging others, nurturing others, guiding others, and creating the best realm we can for us all to thrive in and be the best we can.

So my friends, I ask you to look at your values, and write them down in front of you. What are they?

My Values are...

Are they the values your parents had? Are they values you have learnt through your own experiences in life? Do you live by your values? It is very important you consider all this, because values are the core of your being. They come stored within your spirit, your spirit will have very high divine core values, and the higher self will help and guide the human part to connect to these values as you progress on your life's journey and start to live by them.

For those of you who work with us in the spirit realm, or are starting on your spiritual path, you will start to recognise how your values will change. A simple example of this is what we have seen recently around our friend. Through meditation and Reiki healing, one of her clients has linked with spirit in a basic way, and has started to change her values. She now observes nature more, and rescues insects that she would normally ignore or hurt; she takes more notice now of the world around her, she now pulls away more from people who are unkind, and gives out more kindness to those around her. Now, this is a very simple first connection; as spirit touched her, she realised there is more to her way of being and has taken the first step towards ascending.

Imagine how you could change, my friends, if you completely connect with us, understand and trust us with no fear; what a wonderful life you humans could have. You would have wonderful, divine values to live by and you would nurture everything around you and give love and kindness out to all. A similar new type of loving energy would be drawn to you, my friends, and you would shed the negativity around you.

So look at your values; are they worth having, or do you think you need to change them towards a more love and light way of being? Try and live by your values every day, keep a list of them nearby so you can be reminded of them, because it is key to your core being that these values are true, and true to yourself, and you live by them as best you can.

Wisdom

Wisdom, my friends, is something you come to earth to find on your life's journey. Wisdom is the balance of how you look at your lives and how you see the world around you. Your earth holds millennia of wisdom; it has absorbed everything nature has thrown at it and the different energies from outside forces, such as off- world beings. Mother Earth has learnt from all of this, and managed to balance herself into an eco-system; she holds great wisdom within all of her energy. This wisdom is sent out into the plants and trees, and those of you who have been luckily enough to work with the elemental realms would have connected with trees; they will tell you their story, my friends, and they will give you messages when you attune to the tree spirit.

When you look at an old oak tree, you feel its magic and strength as it stands tall and proud; and as you feel the power that comes through to your inner spirit, you can feel the wisdom it holds. The trees hold many layers of history that are etched within its rings; it has an elemental nature spirit, and elementals that are attached to this tree.

We look forward to more of you being in touch with this side of your world, my friends, because when you do connect to this great wisdom of Mother Earth, you will find you are more driven to be more eco-friendly, and help your Mother earth heal from the pollutants of mankind.

The other wisdom we would like to speak about, my friends, is the wisdom you find as a human being – the knowledge you gain from your learning, teachings from your parents, family, education and from every moment of your life. You gain wisdom from the challenges you experience, and those events that fall in your path that you have to overcome. You gain wisdom from the love and the laughter you find, my friends, and this laughter is something we wish for all of you.

All the time, you are taking on wisdom. Many of you probably don't realise that you are actually absorbing all of this information and the wisdom you will one day give out as an adult to a younger being who needs to be educated. Your experience is passed down to them; it can be through words, or showing them how to create something – this is all wisdom, my friends, this is all experience you have gained. You will only teach them the good parts of what you have learnt, you will teach them how to protect themselves and not to fail at what they are trying to achieve. This is wisdom; you have already learnt and accessed in your own mind and your physical body has experienced, and you will automatically extract the good to teach and pass on to others.

You can also find great wisdom in the elderly on your earth. Many of them are shut away behind doors in a lonely state, with not many younger beings to talk to. But we tell you, my friends, if you could only listen to them and open your ears to their experiences and their lives, you would be amazed at the wisdom you would gain from this. A lot of them have experienced terror and war; these generations are slowly fading for mankind, there are not many of them left with the memories of the great world wars. Much information has not been recorded of the experience and wisdom they gained, and it will be lost in your timeline. We are trying to help mankind record as much as it can, because it is your future generations that will learn from these past experiences, my friends, and how not to let these wars happen again. So if you have an old relative, take the time to ask them about their life, respect them and learn from their wisdom, and record their memories as you listen.

We still see wars in your world, most are based in religion, and we are trying hard to eradicate these wars from your world, to see if mankind can live as one. Different cultures can live side-by-side and we wait for the moment when the wisdom of man can accelerate for them to accept this. When this starts to happen, you will find your different cultures will slowly start to merge into one single culture, with a single belief in the one god, the spirit, and the divine love we hope you will all seek and find on earth. We see no reason why the cultures created over thousands of years on earth cannot retain their essence, but mankind needs to shed the fear-based belief systems so all cultures see they can live under one big umbrella – supporting and loving their neighbours.

So, my friends, every second and every moment of your life you are gaining wisdom. Assess your situations, take the good from them and learn, shed the bad and the fears, then go forward on your life's journey with this wisdom hidden in your memories for you to draw on, build on and teach others from.

Many of you will do this without realising it, my friends, but we do praise you, laugh with happiness and sing with delight in the spirit realm when we see this happening for you. It is a great way for Mother Earth to grow and become what she needs to be.

X Factor

X is the one letter in your western world English language that we had difficulty finding a suitable word to reflect a message from spirit. Then we found the word X Factor we liked this word as it has a little bit of fun around it and this was a word we could use to express some of our thoughts.

So why the X Factor, my friends? The X Factor is a word created by man to reflect someone who is very talented and stands out from the crowd, a talent that lies within, and the creativity of the inner spirit. A lot of you think, *'I'm not a creative person'*, *'I don't have a musical note in my body'*, *'I cannot draw, I cannot paint'*; look at all the negativity in those sentences. Every human has creativity and talent in them. It could be the way you write or even the way you think, but you all have something you can share with your loved ones and your fellow mankind. This sits within you and your ego suppresses it, and it is easy for you to hide behind your ego that says, *'I do not have any talent or anything to give.'* It is easy for you to live your life this way, you don't have to put yourself out there for ridicule, you don't have to face challenges or failure. We would even go as far as to say you don't have to face success, because we see a lot of you living in the fear of being successful and the changes it could make to the life you are living at the moment, so you cocoon yourselves in the ego's protective bubble. You might secretly dream of this, but we see a lot of mankind put up their own barriers, which stop them fulfilling their potential to achieve success.

You are a spirit that walks the earth's path, my friends; you are here to live to your full potential. To the spirit realm, you all have the X Factor; the X Factor to us is that divine spark that sits within you. Your spirit within has the capability of achieving great things, and if you recognise the spirit within and the spirit around you, all sorts of magical things can unfold for you. We would like to take you back to our book 'Utopia', where we made you aware of how some of your great talented humans like Leonardo De Vinci have tapped into the knowledge pot of the Universe. Humans like him found great wisdom and have brought forth things ahead of their time for mankind, but mankind has not always been ready for it. You are now at a point in your ascension where you can tap into this knowledge pot more and more, and mankind will be more accepting of what it has to offer, and will be in awe of what mankind can achieve.

This X Factor lives within you all, you all have something to give. It can be kindness, leadership, teaching and motherhood — these are all creative and require talent. Talent is just not the arts, and you are all good at different things. Never compare yourself with another, my friends, as you are unique, you are YOU. You have your own X Factor, your own sparkle and shine to give out to others.

So don't let your ego stop you fulfilling your potential, bring your X Factor out into the world, let others see you, hear you; place yourself on life's stage, let them applaud you and praise you. But always remember, don't let this go to your head, stay true to yourself and be the best you can be at all times, living in the love and light.

You

You, my friends, YOU are what matters. You are here for a reason as we have already said, to travel a path to discover the love, light and the divine while on your earth's journey. We would love you to live in the ethos of the spirit realm way of being, and to give this out to others around you so they can learn as well.

But to achieve all this, my friends, you have to be at the best you can be, you have to be mentally well, healthy within your physical body, and spiritually at peace with your faith and your religion.

We would all like mankind to be of the spiritualist faith, but we know this is a massive task to ask at this time in mankind's history, and we also know within ourselves that when all your cultures worship their gods, it is actually the divine source they are worshiping.

We do hear all of your thoughts, prayers and wishes, so we embrace mankind as a whole, but what we would like to say is that we embrace you individually as well, my friends. Each one of you matters just as much as the next, and we want you to remember this when you look in your mirrors and you see your reflection that it is YOU that matters.

You might be part of a massive universe, my friends, but every single individual is here for a purpose, you have a reason for being, and you are as important as the next person. We don't want you ever let another human being make you feel devalued and to us you are all equal in our eyes – remember this is in your heart.

You are all here to learn and love and when you come back home to us, you are embraced back into the spirit realm. Whatever life you have lived you are healed, and we take what you have learnt, the bits that are needed for our knowledge pot are kept, and the rest is left to go back into the energy field of the universe.

So live the best, most healthy life you can, and then teach this way of being to your children. Let your children become the individuals they need to be, bring them up to realise they need to be at their best to achieve the best

128

love and kind existence they can be, in their lives, and for others.

Remember it is YOU that matters.

Zest

Zest is a word that is an energy-giving word for you. Some of you know it as the zest of fruit, but to us it is the zest of life. Imagine the moment when you bite into your citrus fruit, a juicy lemon, and you get that bitter tang, but then your senses adjust to its flavour and its goodness, and your body accepts the flavours that come from the zest of the fruit. From its goodness, your senses are raised, as well as your energy levels, my friends.

So we would like to talk about the word zest as an energy-giving word. We want you to go out into your world and live a full life on earth, living the best life you can achieve. Even if you are not able-bodied, and you have a disablement in your life, my friends, you can still go out and live the best life you can.

We want you to find that zest in your life; we want the bitterness to fade away and you to simply enjoy the wonderful goodness that life can bring you. Don't let obstacles stand in your way, see these as challenges, don't let excuses stop you from achieving this in your life.

As we reach the end of this alphabet chapter with the word zest, we know you can achieve this in your life from everything we have written before, you just have to absorb it and believe in yourself, my friends. Have no judgement, don't judge others, don't judge yourself, just know you have done your best; that is all you need to know.

Also be aware, my friends, that it is OK to ask others to help you to achieve the best in your life, as some of you might need this support. We do see the pride of mankind stopping themselves from doing this at times, but why do this to yourselves when a loving hand willingly given from another being could help you fulfil your best potential as you can help others fulfil theirs.

So peel back the layers of that chosen fruit, my friends, and sink your teeth into the zest of its life-giving flesh; feel the strength of its energy, which will give you the life force you need to live a full, loving happy life.

Chapter 6

Magical Inspiration and Guidance from the Spirit Realm

The twist of time

The twist of time as it spins like a star in the sky; it falls and unwinds like a tight coil coming down with the divine.

It touches you within your heart, within your spirit, and as you unwind and spin with time you find you are renewed.

Your path lies on a tunnel of divine love, turning and twisting through the universe as it heads towards us, and as you follow this journey within, you will find your beginning.

The clocks are turning, the time is twisting, it bends back and forth, and you are flexible with this within your spirit - you know its worth.

Follow the twists and bends of time, to find your hope, love and the divine.

Your faith will bring you back to us, back to the place of love.

The raindrop

Water is the transparency of life, reflecting all it sees in its inner self.

The strength you seek lies within this life-giving force of nature.

The power of the wave that can knock you off balance in body.

The serenity of stillness reflecting the blue sky calms your mind.

A single drop of this life-giving force starts new beginnings for all.

One drop reflecting its world around you, look inside this power.

This drop has no foes, only knows the divine life force from above.

Touch the raindrop, absorb its pureness of energy, and reflect.

The single drop is part of a large universal force, calling you to watch.

Stand out in the rain and be cleansed, as it cleanses Mother Nature.

The single raindrop reflects you, your body and inner spirit.

It mirrors the divine love and light you hold in your heart.

Connection from within

Take your mind and look within. What do you see?

Do you see the mist of times gone by lying within?

Do you see sunbeams breaking through the clouds?

Do you see a beautiful existence of love and light?

Do you see shadows and flickers of distant hope?

Do you see doubt and a lost spirit within?

To find what lies within your inner being, you need to sit in the silence, my friends, and focus on your inner essence and spirit. Your spirit within carries its history all for you to rediscover while on this earth plane. When you connect truly to this inner being that lives within you, all the shadows, doubts and mistrust will be forgotten. The light will shine, bouncing you forward on your true path to find kindness, love and the faith of the divine.

Remember, as you connect to your inner being, we are all here celebrating, with you, only a touch away for guidance and the love you need while on this exciting journey on earth.

Celebrate, my friends, your wonderful journey with spirit, and take this out to the world, teach and inspire so others can connect with the spirit being that lies within.

The smile

The magic of the human smile can break down all the barriers.

A smile reflects your true inner self, the truth of the moment.

The smile of the lips and the smile in your eyes you cannot hide.

The knowing smile, the satisfied smile, the smile of contentment, the shy smile, the bright smile, the first kiss smile, the loving smile and the magic of your first smile.

A smile can change someone else's day for the better.

Be that smile that changes the world and beyond.

The magic of the light within

Look within for the light that shines bright.

Like a sun, high in the sky above the clouds.

Rising and setting with each beautiful day.

Others shield their eyes as you shine so bright.

As they get used to your newfound light.

They warm to your light's soft, magic glow.

Let them absorb your warmth and strength.

You are their new teacher and mentor.

Watch their light glow like the stars above.

The magic of the light is within you all.

This divine light never switches off or fades.

Your flame travels with you on all your journeys.

The many journeys you take are lit like a torch.

Your flame grows brighter with knowledge and wisdom.

You are a beacon on a mountaintop, shining out.

Others will be drawn and guided by your light.

You know this and feel the magic of spirit within.

Now sparkle your magic light into your world and beyond.

Do not doubt or hold back, shine bright, my friends.

The magic of the sunrise

As the sun rises in the stillness of the morn,

Mother Earth takes a breath of the divine.

The light shining across the lands,

Awaking all life old and to be born.

The silence is awakened by the light beams.

The chorus of life sings out again to you.

The stillness now has movement and a voice.

Your heart is awakened to Mother Earth's tune.

As the sun rises into the protection of the earth,

Your spirit stretches out to feel its warmth.

Your body absorbs its life-giving energy.

You find your path and life's worth.

As the sun sinks slowly below the horizon,

The silence falls again on your inner being.

Know, my friends, you can hear our voice.

In the silence there is love held frozen.

Sit in the silence and listen.

Hear the night sound of the universe.

Connect to the divine light beams.

You will shine, sparkle and glisten.

Touched by an earth angel

Frightened, lonely, holding in the pain, waiting for the day freedom is gained.

Longing for a spirit of your kind, to stop and gently touch you with love.

The days of endless grind, lack of the divine sits inside your mind.

You rock to and fro with hopelessness, wondering when the pain will go.

You hear a gentle footstep beside you; a hand rests on you, the touch of an angel.

Peace is within your grasp; a further journey lies ahead before freedom is found.

The sun drops, there are new smells and gentle spirits on this new path.

At sunrise your life of chains fades away and your freedom has been gained.

You now have bliss within your heart, touched by love and kindness of others.

You have been touched by earth angels and now walk amongst the green grass.

No more tears, just a smile and the new spirits of your kind in your heart.

Best friends

The physical form holds the strength of Mother Earth, made up from the elements of life itself.

The physical body holds the source of the divine pure love from beyond, your shell of energy wrapping itself like a cocoon around your spirit friend within.

Your spirit friend lies protected in your human form, connecting to all of you from within and beyond.

Joy is beheld as you travel your journey together on Mother Earth, like best friends on an adventure to bring love and kindness and a higher way of being to the earth plane.

There is no sadness on the day these friends separate forever, only joy is found.

The physical form has served its purpose and Mother Earth accepts you back into her bosom.

Your spiritual friend, YOU, travels back home to pick up on your spirit life you had before your earth journey.

Your physical life is never forgotten, the human essence living on in your spirit with the knowledge and wisdom gained while here on earth.

Remember, forever blessed, forever wiser and loved beyond words at all times – while joined together and separated at death of the physical form, your light will always shine.

Finding Harmony

Harmony lies within you like a flower bud waiting to open, it waits to be released on your earth life's path. When the flower blooms the pollen is released and will swirl round you, cocooning and protecting you from the fears and the doubts you have about yourself and the world around you.

Harmony is a friend; it protects you from the unknown; when found it sets you on the track of life; remember you are born with harmony within from the moment you take your first breath.

To sustain the harmony you crave, my friends, you need to look at your life, the balance of love against fear, trust against doubt and to manifest what you desire in your life through positive thought.

Harmony can be achieved, my friends, take the simple moment when you watch a bee buzzing above a flower to collect pollen, imagine the wings slow down and you see the bee in a moment of time held in suspension, this is a perfect moment of harmony.

Harmony is when you feel peace and calmness within, a happiness that can never fade. This sits within you all my friends; it is only a touch away. Spirit is harmony, we live in harmony, in love and trust, and this can all be yours.

Some of you see this as out of reach, beyond far horizons; you might see this as a challenge to achieve in the turmoil of your life. But if you could just sit and take your time, and the moments needed sitting listening to the world around by tuning into Mother Nature, the spirit realm and beyond, then you will start to find that balance within, my friends.

Once you have that balance within you, it will trigger the harmony you seek. The harmony of a calm mind that does not judge others, does not criticize, that accepts what comes and trusts that all will be good and well. The harmony of the body, health, the nourishment balance of food and water, this is all vital to creating the harmony you need, my friends.

Once you find the harmony within, the turmoil, the friction, the doubts, the non-believers, the ridiculers will sit at your boundary, they will no longer affect you or hurt you, they will exist with you and be part of your lives, but they cannot harm you. You have found the harmony we create, the

141

protection you need to carry on with your spiritual journey.

As you progress on this journey you are taking, my friends, the harmony you have now found will be seen by others; there will be jealousy, as we have said, people will recoil from you, but then others will be drawn to you. This is all part of your journey, your journey of finding harmony within you.

The key thing for you is when you find this harmony and acceptance of who you are and the balance of health and life, you will be able to reflect this out to others, it will become part of your teachings, part of your way of being. You will find others will wish to be as you are, living in harmony.

Everything you have learnt in this life has come to this stage of your journey and will be what you can teach to others, the good and the bad of your experiences and how to balance themselves. Tell others how you felt when you first experienced spirit, tell your stories, my friends, you will be surprised how people will want to listen to you. They will want to hear your wisdom and philosophy to balance their lives, as they are seeking harmony themselves. They will not realise this at first, but their inner spirit knows this and is trying to encourage them with their higher self in the spirit realm to seek this harmony.

So reflect and realise that just one simple word from you can change someone's life, and as you reflect your harmony out to others you will become more balanced, more rested within yourself, and you will be in the harmony state that you need to walk your path in life, my friends.

Live in beautiful harmony, rested, peaceful and trusting and with the divine light within you, and you will have wonderful lives.

Heal yourself

The healing you seek starts from within and then reaches up to the divine. The good intent of the healer will channel the love and the touch of God as they rest their hands on you.

Open your heart up to this wonderful healing source so you can feel its strength. This is the strength of the divine that you need to trigger your healing process.

Open your mind and heart to accepting that all will be well, and give over to us any anger, fears, doubt and trust, as you will be whole again.

Your mind holds the key to successful healing; you know you block your progress. Imagine yourself well, running free in Mother Nature, pain-free and loved.

With the combination of your freed mind and the healing touch of the divine, you will be released from your health restrictions and be able to live the life you desire.

Sparkles on the waves

Imagine you are sitting quietly on the beach, watching the sun sparkle and glisten on the water. Your mind drifts away with the tide, as the waves lap on the shore.

Where are you going? Are you drifting away from your earth? Drifting far beyond, to a divine existence of pure love and joy.

You reach your destination and are standing on the tip of a far horizon. Will you step over this new reality or turn around and go back?

As you hesitate, an old friend's hand draws you into a world of peace and tranquillity. You are in awe of the beauty and magic this place holds.

Everything you touch sparkles and glistens, you feel the touch of the divine and are at peace. But there is a distant sound of lapping water on the shore calling you back.

The tide has come in and is washing over your feet and time is forgotten. Was it a dream or did I just touch the magic of the divine?

New Horizons

While on your life's journey on earth and in the spirit realm, there will be opportunities placed in your path. Look at these opportunities as improving yourselves, my friends, improving your skills, your mental mind, physical body and your being as a whole.

Don't be afraid to go towards a new horizon that is shining before you like a beacon of light, and as you reach that horizon, don't be afraid of the next horizon, as there will be many through your life's path.

Many of you wait for the sun to rise and fall again before you make decisions; sometimes decisions need to be made quicker, so you do not miss the opportunities that are placed before you.

When you start to awaken to the spirit realm and see the sun shining brightly and the stars in the heavens, and we come knocking on your door, the spirit realm places opportunities and signs near and far on your horizon.

As you connect with us you will gain confidence; the new horizons will never be a problem for you, you will always reach them. The new opportunities you set yourself and we set before you, will not be a challenge to you they will be an adventure, my friends. They will be an adventure to help you complete your whole self while here on earth.

So take these opportunities, with out fear, only trust, and trust that you are sailing towards the right horizon.

The Dark Shadow Within

Our wish is for your body to be born pure and cleansed surrounded by love. Your body cleansed of any darkness and substances, which your world could harm it by.

There are those mothers nurturing the fetus among mankind that take harmful substances that affect the baby's body and inner spirit. But when these babies are born we try to cleanse them of the substances so their path in life can be clean and wholesome again.

These substances come from your Mother Earth, which could be used for healing if used correctly amongst mankind. But the drug warlords among man still have the greed and hunger for wealth taking these substances and sell them among you to cause harm and darkness in the light. There is no discrimination for them who they sell it to and the humans that get caught up in this drug world.

The human body and mind is so strongly affected by this abuse they inflict on themselves, they see no reasoning and commit acts through desperation to full fill their addiction. Their acts of great unkindness cause great pain against their fellow man. They push their loved ones to the furthest boundaries and put up a wall so they can't get in.

But you must remember my friends that these humans need help; no matter what atrocities they cause through substance abuse they need your help. They need to be bought back from the brink from where their body can no longer be abused any more and to stop the hurt they cause others while on this path, to bring them back from the loneliness they feel within.

Their inner spirit does not have the strength to fight this type of abuse my friends even with our help. We see their loved ones do everything they can to try and bring their loved ones back from the brink of despair. But the substances and the dark shadows in the world that push these drugs for wealth, out weigh the single factor of the love of the loved ones.

Once the human has taken drugs they are easy targets and dragged back in

146

to that life of despair again, their mind has been weakened and they look for away to forget the dark shadow within them.

We see this is a massive problem all over your world and causes us great sadness. We see the individual who think their lives are unhappy, or are mentally not coping, seeking a release from these feelings, which at the start the substance they chose gives them. It gives them the kick to make them smile and feel good again and this is how it all starts my friends, the spiral of the drugs, alcohol and despair for that single human and all that love them.

If only these humans could stand back at those moments in their life's and look at the good things in their life's, if only we could lift that despair from their minds so they don't go down that path. This is not a chosen path my friends for any of you, it is a challenge we see that faces us among you all.

We see the human character can be weak and is influenced by other humans that take you down this path, the weak are targeted by the substance suppliers, who themselves are not users. Remember my friends if you see a child or adult you think is abusing a substance in your lives try to intervene, try to be strong, try and help them. You will hit walls, you will hit barriers but you are the stronger because you are not on the substances that will block your mind and your physical body to the love and light and the divine love that is out there.

These people need your help and not to be shunned, you will not get any thanks back from them my friends, apart from the hope that one day they will live a clean life again. This is part of your ascension, you will give so much and not receive any thing back my friends. The reward will be seeing that human is who they once were and not what they had become.

The Nurtured Child

The child never walks their path of life alone, they are always protected by their mother and father in life and in the spirit realm.

The wings of angels bring them in to this world releasing their care over to you.

You nurture them to the day they spread their wings and leave your loving home. The first stage of your job is completed as their earth guardian angel.

You watch from a far with joy at their achievements, sending them love every second of your day, and holding them in your hearts in times of despair.

A child will always bring you joy and heart ache, but remember my friends to be proud of what you have achieved, the fact they are confident to live their lives as they should.

They will always know your are there to fall back on in times of need and your doors and arms are always open to them.

So smile and release them into your world, we will always be at their side protecting them and guiding them on their life's path. We will call on you when you are needed just listen and look for the signs.

Your are the nurturer of love and the divine and we thank you for the role you have undertaken as carers of our spirit friends and being part of their journeys so far.

Remember you all depart this world and meet in the spirit realm to continue your journeys together, so do not worry of what the future might bring, just enjoy the moments of now.

The Silence

The silent being, alone in the shadows, no light shines in their world. You do not see them; they are hidden behind close doors, shadows of their former selves.

They are seen as loners and ignored by their fellow mankind, look; you can see the sadness in their eyes. Was this isolation living by choice? Some would say yes as it's easier to believe that.

We would say my friends your paths are for love and companion ship with a loving hand reaching out to you in the darkness. Open the closed doors and don't be afraid to step into the shadows.

You can bring love and light to the lonely in your world. Stretch out a helping hand to those living in a silent existence. That loving touch will bring them forward into the light out of the shadows and chatter of companionship.

The Journey of Knowledge

A jump   A skip   A step

How are you moving forward with the next stage of your journey on earth?

A stride   A leap   A climb

Do you have the faith and trust to take the next step?

A look   A glance   A smile

Observe all a round you so you can make the positive choices you need to take for the next part of your journey on your life's path.

Listen   Trust   Faith

You have your spirit friends to guide you and all the answers you seek lay within you.

Connect   Love   Give

Go forward without hesitation and follow your life's path to the light.

Divine   God   Universe

The answers you seek are in reach, look, listen and observe, it is all within your grasp.

Enjoy *Blessed* *Home*

Now sit back and enjoy the ride on earth knowing you are protected until you return back to us.

Teaching *Inspired* *Learn*

Your journey of gaining knowledge will carry on in the spirit realm and you are always learning and ascending to the light of the divine.

Spirit *Angel* *Realm*

The love of the divine awaits you, stay safe in the knowledge you are loved and guided back to us to take the next steps on your spirit journey of knowledge and learning.

The Beauty of the Morning

As the beauty of the morning dawns on yet another day, your world responds like a flower opening up its petals to the morning warmth of the rays of the sun.

Your spirit is ready for this next day, the next step on its path on this journey, while walking along in the warmth and the light that the sun gives your Mother Earth.

Enjoy the beauty my friends, enjoy the song of nature, look into the depths of your oceans as there is beauty hidden everywhere on your planet.

But take yourself also to the dark parts of your world where there are depths of despair still and pollution that is hidden from the human eye.

These parts of the world have not yet found the beauty and the light that opens that flower every morning that responds to the sun and lives it life as it should.

You can all help with prayer, positive thoughts, good will, and acts of kindness to change the world you are living in.

Would it not be a wonderful thing for every human being to wake up and see the beauty of the morning, not knowing any fear or dread of the day ahead, and they only ever experience love and kindness.

All humans would then be embraced with love and light and be able to fulfill your life's to its best potential, giving and receiving so much love, imagine what your world could be like my friends.

Imagine the beauty of the morning every day, every minute of your day, every second of your day, that feeling of wonder as you take in that morning breath of freshness of the earths dew.

So we say to you my friends take these thoughts and spread love and light out in to your world to every human being and see the beauty that lies within mankind.

Reflection in the Lake

Imagine the majestic earth mountains, pine forests and lakes, you are sitting at the waters edge on a completely calm beautiful summers day.

The stillness of the moment, a captured picture of time held in the minds eye.

The earth, the sky and the inner spirit are reflected in to the depth of the lake.

You are held still by the beauty and wonder of this moment, if only it could carry on for ever, only being disturbed by the birds over head and the song of nature.

A silent ripple catches your eye and brings you back to your existence in time, moving you forward with your future thoughts.

These moments of serenity have helped you leave your past behind, your mind now reflecting on the wonder of what could be.

Walk back into your busy worlds, but always hold that moment of peace and calmness in your hearts to draw on when needed.

Reflection is a form of healing, look deep in to the pools of water, search your spirit within for the answers and ask us to guide you to find that inner peace in your life.

Song of the Divine

Listen to the music my friends, the beat of the song.

The notes of life that flow along the rhythm of time.

The message that is in the words connects with your heart.

Listen to the music of nature, the tune on the wings in flight.

The melody of the grasses swaying in the summer breeze.

The chorus of notes with the rising dawn on the horizon.

Listen to your angel's song, of love and the divine.

The soft enchanting tunes of the melody of the heavens above.

Let them resonate through your inner spirit and beyond.

All music is from love my friends and comes from a higher source.

Your heart and spirit sings when it connects with a tune of love.

Live on that wave of divine music and sing out your love to the world.

The Angel Hug

As the angels take the one you love from earth boundaries, they travel home to the heavenly realms.

Their physical form is laid to rest celebrating their life at it's best.

Don't worry my friend they are safe in our arms, they're journey continues in the heavenly realms.

Let the sadness fall away and remember the happy days.

Place a smile on your face and remember their grace.

They will always stay true to you and the love you knew.

As you travel your path of life and love, remember my friend they are always there giving you that angel hug.

Now let go of the sadness and remember the love and one day you will meet in heaven above.

TRUST

Trust in your spiritual path my friends and know that you are all where you are supposed to be at this moment in your time.

Do not analyse, doubt or question, just trust that all you are experiencing at this time is what you need at this moment on your life's journey. We will give you messages with guidance and signs to pick up on. If you do not understand the messages or signs do not let your ego over analyse them, as this way you will miss the door that we are trying to open for you. Step back and ask us to send another sign or message that is clearer and you will understand. Listen to your *intuition* that is a gift from us, if you feel this is weak you need to meditate more and get to know your inner self and this will help you to trust this gift that sits within you.

As you know we are not human, we have to interact and connect with you through layers of the earths energy and your own, some days this harder than others. Also for yourself you will have days where emotions, or health can affect you hearing us correctly or seeing our signs. None of us are perfect and we have to work at our relationship with each other and we are all trying for the greater good for mankind to achieve a better loving existence.

Remember take one step at a time, make sure you are clear on the message you have received and fully understood the signs, this way we will achieve great things by working together in the divine love and light.

We thank you, my friends

The journey of mankind so far has been very fascinating for us in the spirit realm. It has been a pleasure and a privilege to be part of this with you, and see what your earth has developed into so far.

We have said in books how much better we wish you to be as a race of beings, but what we would also like to say to you, my friends, is we are very proud of what you have all achieved so far. When the spirit joins the human body it is not an easy journey for us, as the human is unaware of this joining. For the human side of you to recognise that there is something else beyond the human form is quite an achievement, my friends, and we must give you credit for this.

As you progress through your next few centuries, more and more of mankind will recognise the spirit realm and that you have a spirit within. You will see that we are here to guide and protect you, and help you achieve the best you can while on this earth's journey for mankind.

So, my friends, we would like to applaud you all for what you have achieved. It has been over many, many, many centuries that you have progressed to the point you are at now. Each individual human is unique with their own purpose, but remember, my friends, all your journeys are intertwined and woven together for greater purpose. With our pure love way of being and all-knowing in the spirit realm, we can plan this interaction with you all.

Nearly all your lifetime interactions with fellow humans, animals and places would have been planned. But as we said earlier in this book, some of these interactions can be unplanned, because with all the best intentions we may have in the spirit realm, we cannot get it right one hundred percent of the time.

But back to you, my friends, back to all of YOU, we would like you to pat yourselves on the back for what mankind has achieved so far. Forget your wars, forget the dark areas of your world and the areas still neglected, bring to the forefront the positives, the people who are striving to make the changes on your Mother Earth, these are the people we wish to applaud. These people are the ones who are going to take what they have learnt and teach this to your world, and help the ones still in darkness to move forward to the light.

So remember, every achievement you make, my friends, is for the benefit of yourselves and future generations of mankind; it is not for the benefit of us in the spirit realm, it is for yourselves. This is what you must remember, that it is you who are important in all of this. Yes, we do learn from you, gain knowledge and wisdom that helps our development too, but to us, it's you the individuals, and your world as a whole that is important.

And as other beings in the universe wait and watch, they send blessings to you as well, giving you confidence to make those strides that mankind can to move forward into a higher ascended way of being. So thank you again, my friends, and we look forward to our long continued journey with the human race, and you as individuals.

Love and blessings to you all. xxxxxxx

ABOUT THE AUTHOR

Sharon Bengalrose is a medium and holistic healer based in Newport, South Wales (UK). Through her work with spirit, she loves to help people de-stress, find happiness and raise their positive energy levels with messages and healing. Her third book, **'The magic of Spirit**, is written in partnership with her spirit team. This book has followed on from a previous joint adventure with her guides, 'Utopia' and 'Inspiration Guidance cards and book' .

Visit her website www.bengalrose.co.uk to find out more. You will also find her on twitter @SBengalrose and facebook https://www.facebook.com/Bengalrosehealing/.

Made in the USA
Middletown, DE
21 May 2017